STANDING FOR TRUTH

An Introduction to Apologetics

EDITED BY MATT DAMICO

ILLUSTRATED BY DAN DEWITT

CROSSINGS PRESS 2018

TABLE OF CONTENTS

t hings change. You change, your family changes, your job, school, and friends all change sometimes. This is all normal and good, mostly. We're dynamic creatures living in a dynamic world, so we should not expect life to be stagnant.

But there are exceptions. For example, look at what the Apostle Paul said to a group of Christians two thousand years ago: "So then, brothers, *stand firm* and *hold to* the traditions that you were taught by us, either by our spoken word or by our letter" (2 Thessalonians 2:15).

Paul told them to "stand firm" and "hold to" the things they'd been taught. That's basically the same thing as saying, "don't change." What does he mean by that?

Well, he certainly *doesn't* mean that those Thessalonians should never grow or progress in maturity and Christlikeness. What he means is that the Christian faith and tradition is something that is handed down from generation to generation, and each generation is responsible to hold on to it and push against any distortion.

If you pay any attention to what's going on in American culture right now, you know that opinions and "facts" can change in just a moment. And you're probably aware of the increasing pressure on Christians to change their minds on things that the Bible makes clear. How should Christians respond to such pressure? By standing firm.

Why can't we just let the truth "evolve," as some people claim it does? Why can't we just let go of aspects of biblical truth that seem out of step with the world around us? Because the truth doesn't belong to us. The Bible says that "there is no variation or shadow due to change" in God (James 1:17). He is always and ever true; what is true of him now has always been true of him. Unlike us, God does not change, and his truth does not shift. So we stand firm, and we commit to knowing and cherishing the truth of God's Word.

If you're going to stand for truth, you need to know the truth, and you've got to be "prepared to make a defense to anyone who asks you for a reason for the hope that is in you" (1 Peter 3:15).

We're thrilled about this book, because it's going to help you do just that. This book will guide you through questions you're going to face as a Christian: questions about the Bible, about Jesus, and more. You'll learn from trustworthy writers how to answer those questions, and you'll be introduced to important people from the past who have valiantly stood for truth.

My hope is that, as you read this book, our never–changing–God will use his never–changing–truth to change you into a bold witness for him.

FOR THE TRUTH,
MATT DAMICO
CROSSINGS MINISTRIES

Introduction

BY R. ALBERT MOHLER JR.

t hese are challenging times for Christian young people. The historical context in which you live puts you in proximity of an unprecedented diversity of worldviews. The religious diversity, and the significant segment of young people who identify with no religion – the "nones" – make this a unique, and uniquely challenging, time to be a Christian.

But that is not all. The increase in religious pluralism and secularism around us has been accompanied by an increase in hostility toward those who claim Christ as Lord. Indeed, the faith of more and more young Christians is being challenged and put on the defense.

The question for you, then, is whether you will be ready to give such a defense. It is not a matter of *if* the time will come for you to explain why you believe what you believe, but *when*. Each of us will eventually be required to "contend for the faith once for all delivered to the saints" (Jude 3). Our responsibility as Christians – young and old – is to be ready.

These times call for you to use your mind and think – about what you believe, about what others believe, and why people believe what they believe. This is what is required for you to love the Lord your God with all your mind (Matthew 22:37) and to take every thought captive to Christ (2 Corinthians 10:5).

The fact that you're holding this book is a good sign that you understand the task before you. And it's a good sign that you want to be ready "to make a defense to anyone who asks you for a reason for the hope that is in you" (1 Peter 3:15). This defense of the faith is known as apologetics, and that's what this book is about. Read this book carefully, and you'll be ready to stand for the truth of God, even as alternative worldviews gain traction around us.

There are multiple ways to give a defense for the Christian faith. One way is to marshal different lines of evidence that explain why Christianity is true, often appealing to outside sources to support the claims of Christianity.

Knowing different reasons and lines of evidence that backup the biblical narrative is immensely helpful. It is good and necessary to remind ourselves and those who oppose us that the best of science and history serve to bolster, not weaken, the Christian worldview.

But we also must admit that no amount of evidence can change someone's heart. All who are separated from God are, the Bible says, dead in their trespasses and sins (Ephesians 2), tainting even their rational capacities and ability to perceive the world. To make a dead man live requires nothing less than a new creation and a Holy Spirit induced new birth.

The Apostle Paul tells us that all people know that God is real. He has made his power and divinity clear to all people (Romans 1:19–20). The problem is that people suppress this truth and live godless lives. This truth should give you great confidence as you give a defense of the faith. For every person you talk to – even if they claim no religious identity, and even if they claim there is no god – knows deep down that God is there. So be ready to let the truth of God speak into this point of contact you have with every unbeliever.

In addition to equipping you to articulate your beliefs, studying apologetics is good for the Christian soul. As Christians of all ages, we ought to ask ourselves regularly whether we really believe what we say we believe. A healthy Christian faith asks the most important questions – like those you'll find in this book – with full confidence in a biblical answer. We of all people ought to hold our convictions with confidence that our God is real and that he has spoken authoritatively.

The Christian faith has faced challenges since the opponents of Jesus tried to conceal his resurrection. But here we are two thousand years later. The risen Lord still reigns, and the number of his followers continues to grow. The Christian faith, resting on the Lord Jesus and on his holy Word, has withstood two millennia of opposition, and you can be sure that is not going to change. Jesus promised that the gates of hell would not prevail against his people, and that's a guarantee with no expiration date. So prepare to stand against the tide, and do it with confidence.

Read on, read with pen in hand, read with curiosity, joy, and confidence in the truth of God. Bind yourself to God's Word, for his truth alone will set you free.

> The Christian faith, resting on the Lord Jesus and on his holy Word, has withstood two millennia of opposition, and you can be sure that is not going to change. Jesus promised that the gates of hell would not prevail against his people, and that's a guarantee with no expiration date.

PART ONE

The Foundation for Christianity

01

The
Bible

WHAT IS IT?

BY MAC BRUNSON

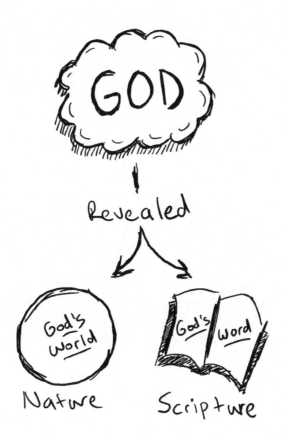

01

following the Reformation, a flood of error swept over Europe that would influence the continent and the world for centuries. That flood of error was rationalism. The age of enlightenment had dawned, glorifying man's reason and the findings of science. This flood was intent on sweeping away the authority of God's Word.

Over the years, there has been one attack on the Bible after another, with criticism leveled against the Word of God and its origination, inception, and credibility. Almost all arguments against the Bible arise from the assumption that the Bible must have corroborating evidences from extra–biblical sources. In other words, the Bible is guilty and must be proven at every point to be innocent.

Yet through the centuries, the Bible has withstood all attacks and outlasted all opponents. When you pick up a Bible, you are holding the most important and enduring book in all the world. More than any other book, it is has transformed human history.

What makes the Bible so unique? To answer that, I want to cover three elements that help us understand just what the Bible is. There's more that could be said, but these are vital.

I. Revelation

The Bible is divine revelation. There is a God, and he has chosen to reveal himself through the Bible. There are two types of revelation: general revelation and special revelation. In general revelation, God reveals himself to us through the created order. Paul writes in Romans 1:20:

> For his invisible attributes, namely, his eternal power and divine nature, have been clearly perceived, ever since the creation of the world, in the things that have been made. So they are without excuse.

General revelation was never intended to supply all that God wanted us to know about himself and his will for our lives. God created us, and he created us to have fellowship with him. God came, we are told, in the cool of the day and walked the garden with Adam and Eve. However, sin entered the world through man's rebellion and disobedience, and that daily communication was shattered. Sin separated a holy God from fallen man.

God began to communicate with man in other ways, ways that can be called special revelation. In the Old Testament, you read about God communicating his will to the priest through the Urim and the Thummim (Exodus 28:30; Numbers 27:21). God used dreams (Genesis 20:3), visions (Isaiah 6:1), and theophanies (Exodus 3:2) to communicate with specific men at specific times. There were angels (Daniel 9:20–21; Luke 2:10–11), prophets, and events to speak to his people.

The greatest act of communication came with Jesus Christ, the living Word of God. The writer of Hebrews states in Hebrews 1:1–2:

> Long ago, at many times and in many ways, God spoke to our fathers by the prophets, but in these last days he has spoken to us by his Son.

Special revelation is the way God communicated his Word to us:

> The secret things belong to the Lord our God, but the things that are revealed belong to us and to our children forever, that we may do all the words of this law. (Deuteronomy 29:29)

We can know of God's existence through natural revelation, but we know God's plan of salvation only through his special revelation to man. God's written Word is his special revelation. If we want to know him, we need to know his Word.

QUESTION:

How would you summarize the differences between general revelation and special revelation? What are some examples of general revelation? Where has God revealed himself most clearly to us?

_____

_____

_____

_____

_____

_____

II. Inspiration

The doctrine of inspiration, according to Charles Ryrie, "is not something theologians have forced on the Bible. Rather it is a teaching of the Bible itself." The Bible is full of statements that reveal that it is God's Word and that God inspired certain men to write it. We read in 2 Timothy 3:16–17:

> All Scripture is breathed out by God and profitable for teaching, for reproof, for correction, and for training in righteousness, that the man of God may be complete, equipped for every good work.

That became a matter of conviction for me one evening about midnight, sitting at a desk in the dorm room at Furman University. Taking Classical Greek, I was attempting for the first time to read those verses out of the Greek New Testament. The Greek literally states, "All Scripture God–breathed." In Genesis 2:7 we are told that God breathed into man's nostrils the breath of life, and man became a living soul. In the same way, every word in Scripture came from the mouth of God. Look at how Luke, as a representative of the New Testament writers, views the Old Testament and how it came to us:

> Sovereign Lord, who made the heaven and the earth and the sea and everything in them, who through the mouth of our father David, your

DEFENDERS OF THE FAITH

AUGUSTINE OF HIPPO
B . 354 | D . 430

Augustine of Hippo is widely considered the most influential Christian thinker since the first century. After years of selfish and sinful pursuits, Augustine converted to Christianity in 386 and went on to become the bishop of Hippo in northern Africa. He left an indelible mark on the history of the church with his writings and contributions to theology, philosophy, and more. Some of his enduring works include *The City of God*, *On Christian Doctrine*, and *On the Trinity*.

IF YOU READ ONE BOOK BY AUGUSTINE, MAKE IT: *Confessions*

servant, said by the Holy Spirit, "Why did the Gentiles rage, and the peoples plot in vain? The kings of the earth set themselves, and the rulers were gathered together, against the Lord and against his Anointed." (Acts 4:24–26)

In this passage from Acts, Peter and John quote Psalm 146:6, and then they state that the Holy Spirit gave these words through the mouth of David, and then quoted Psalm 2:1–2.

You see the process of inspiration in Jeremiah 1:9 where we read:

Then the Lord put out his hand and touched my mouth. And the Lord said to me, "Behold, I have put my words in your mouth."

The original writings of the Old and New Testament were breathed out by God to the prophets, the apostles, and all those who penned Scripture.

The question is often raised, "How did that process take place?" Some say it was a "natural" process, that the biblical writers were inspired in the way we speak of Shakespeare or any other masterful writer being inspired. It is clear from the reading of Scripture that the inspiration of the Word of God is different than the way we might describe a Shakespearean sonnet or play to be inspired.

Some hold to a "dynamic" or "mystical" inspiration, where men sat in a trance and wrote Scripture. Some call this the "dictation method." However, it is clear that God used the people, their experiences, and their personalities as they wrote. God did not "possess" them, but through them wrote his Word.

Others hold to "degree inspiration," where Scripture has varying degrees of inspiration. Still others believe in "partial inspiration," where Scripture is inspired in parts. The problem with this is that the decision for which parts are inspired is left up to the fallible reader.

I hold to a "verbal–plenary" view of inspiration. "Verbal" points to the fact that God spoke his Word to those he selected to write Scripture. "Plenary" means that all Scripture is inspired, every part of it in all its parts. It is also my conviction that the Word of God is inerrant – without error – and infallible, which means it is all–sufficient for faith and practice.

Understanding the Bible

Illumination

The Holy Spirit comes to every believer, helping him or her to understand the truth of God's Word.

Revelation

God's written Word is his special revelation. If we want to know him, we need to know his Word.

Inspiration

The original writings of the Old and New Testament were breathed out by God to the prophets, the apostles, and all those who penned Scripture.

QUESTION:

Read these verses from 2 Peter and summarize what it says about Scripture and where it came from.

"No prophecy of Scripture comes from someone's own interpretation. For no prophecy was ever produced by the will of man, but men spoke from God as they were carried along by the Holy Spirit." (2 Peter 1:20–21)

_____

_____

_____

_____

Inspiration does not extend to the writer's thoughts or oral pronouncements, but to the very words themselves. Every word came from God. David in 2 Samuel 23:2 says:

The Spirit of the Lord speaks by me; his word is on my tongue.

Down through the centuries, man has denied and attempted to destroy the Word of God, and yet this coming Sunday, around the world, it will be preached to millions upon millions. It will be used to counsel and console. It will be used to offer direction and encouragement. It will be shared with those who are desperate and in need of salvation because God's inspired Word is still true, still effective, and still God–breathed.

GOD

01

III. Illumination

The Holy Spirit comes to every believer, helping him or her to understand the truth of God's Word. 1 Corinthians 2:10–16 says,

> These things God has revealed to us through the Spirit. For the Spirit searches everything, even the depths of God. For who knows a person's thoughts except the spirit of that person, which is in him? So also no one comprehends the thoughts of God except the Spirit of God. Now we have received not the spirit of the world, but the Spirit who is from God, that we might understand the things freely given us by God. And we impart this in words not taught by human wisdom but taught by the Spirit, interpreting spiritual truths to those who are spiritual.

> The natural person does not accept the things of the Spirit of God, for they are folly to him, and he is not able to understand them because they are spiritually discerned. The spiritual person judges all things, but is himself to be judged by no one. "For who has understood the mind of the Lord so as to instruct him?" But we have the mind of Christ.

It is clear that the Holy Spirit illumines the Word for the believer, but this is not available to those who do not believe. You see, when by faith you put your trust in Jesus Christ as Lord and Savior of your life, the Holy Spirit begins to illumine the Word of God for you. This does not mean you will understand everything you read immediately. It does mean that the Spirit becomes your teacher, instructor, and illuminator of the Word and aids you in grasping God's truth and applying it to your life.

The Scriptures of the Old Testament and New Testament are revelation from God, written by inspiration. You can trust that, as you read, God will give you illumination. Remember the promising words of the psalmist in Psalm 119:130:

> The unfolding of your words gives light; it imparts understanding to the simple.

The glory of God and the Word of God are inseparable. I have no sure sight of God's glory except through his Word. The Word mediates the glory, and the glory confirms the Word.

– John Piper

02

The Bible

HOW WE GOT IT

BY TIMOTHY PAUL JONES

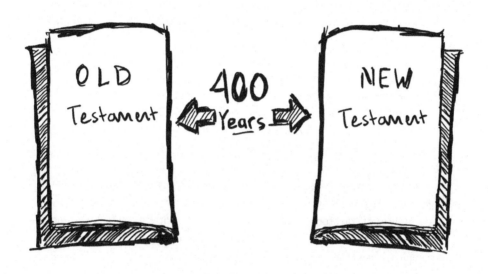

02

t he Bible. One book made up of sixty-six books, two testaments, more than forty authors who together tell the story of the glory of God revealed in Jesus Christ. This book alone is God's written revelation of himself, known in the mind of God before time began. According to the Apostle Peter, people "spoke from God as they were carried along by the Holy Spirit" (2 Peter 1:21). According to Paul, not merely the authors but the text itself was inspired, "breathed out by God" (2 Timothy 3:16).

But how did the Bible get from God to us? How did these words make it from the mind of God to the minds of human beings and then to the book that we hold in our hands today?

How We Got the Old Testament

The first report we have of God calling a human being to write was when God commanded Moses to write what he heard (Exodus 17:14; 24:4–7). And so, Moses recounted the story of God's work with humanity all the way from the beginning of time up to the people's entrance into the promised land.

After the time of Moses, God superintended the lives of prophets and priests, poets and kings, so that they wrote the very words that God intended. They wrote on stone, in plaster, on leather, on papyrus, in Hebrew, and in Aramaic. As their proclamations and prophecies turned out to be true, the people received their words as the very words of God.

Because they viewed these words as the words of God, the people of Israel wanted to preserve these words. From the earliest stages of Israel's history, scribes copied the books of the Old Testament. By the sixth century A.D., a group of scribes known as the Masoretes had refined earlier scribal practices into a set of traditions that carefully maintained the text of the Old Testament; the Masoretes carefully counted every letter of the Old Testament and included special markings throughout every text to preserve the right readings.

Until the mid-twentieth century, many scholars doubted the accuracy of these copies. And yet, when the Dead Sea Scrolls were discovered in 1947, scholars suddenly had access to Old Testament manuscripts hundreds of years older than the oldest text that the Masoretes had preserved! When these older texts were compared with the Masoretic Text, it became clear that — even though there were differences among these manuscripts — the process used by the Masoretes had been a trustworthy process that had reliably preserved the text of the Old Testament.

How does this story – of how the Old Testament Scriptures were written and preserved – influence your confidence in the truthfulness of the Old Testament? Was any of this surprising to you?

_____

_____

_____

_____

The Time Between the Testaments

When the last Old Testament prophet wrote his last inspired words, God's written revelation came to an end — for a time. This silence didn't last for a few months or a few years or even a few decades.

It lasted four hundred years.

But God's story was far from over.

The purpose of God's work in the Old Testament had been to prepare the way for the coming of a Savior who would keep the covenants Israel had broken. Every word of the Old Testament leans forward with eager anticipation in the direction of this Messiah. Those years of silence didn't point to a failure in God's plan; they were God's preparation for the fulfillment of his plan.

The words that God spoke after those years of silence pointed to the coming of Jesus, the true and living Word of God. Jesus never criticized or corrected the Jewish Scriptures. Instead, he fulfilled them and treated them as the true and trustworthy words of his heavenly Father. And then, when he rose from the dead, Jesus demonstrated once and for all that his claims about himself and about the Scriptures were true.

How We Got the New Testament

After Jesus ascended into the heavens, those who had walked and talked with him passed on his teachings and the stories of his life — first in oral histories, then in literary productions recorded in the Greek language.

From the moment that words about Jesus began to be written, Christians received the words of eyewitnesses who had seen the risen Lord Jesus — as well as close associates of these eyewitnesses — as the authoritative words of God.

When Paul said in his second letter to Timothy that the Scriptures were "God-breathed" (2 Timothy 3:16), his words pointed primarily to the Old Testament. After all, when Paul wrote this letter, some New Testament texts probably weren't even finished yet! Yet, even when Paul wrote this letter, Christians were already aware that "Scripture" included not only the Old Testament but also the words of believers who had seen the risen Jesus and close associates of these eyewitnesses.

> **From the moment that words about Jesus began to be written, Christians received the words of eyewitnesses who had seen the risen Lord Jesus — as well as close associates of these eyewitnesses — as the authoritative words of God.**

Two biblical texts make it clear that, even in the first century, Christians were already treating New Testament writings as Scripture:

- In Paul's first letter to Timothy, Paul identified words spoken by Jesus that became part of Luke's Gospel as "Scripture" (compare Luke 10:7 with 1 Timothy 5:18).
- Shortly after Paul wrote his second letter to Timothy, Simon Peter referred to Paul's letters as "Scripture" (2 Peter 3:16).

Despite what many skeptics claim, the writings that became part of the New Testament weren't chosen by any powerful bishop or emperor or church council. They were received as God's Word because they were the trustworthy testimony of people who had either seen Jesus alive or were closely connected to those who had seen Jesus.

Around twenty books of the New Testament were recognized as authoritative from the very beginnings of the Christian faith — and these included the four Gospels and Acts, Paul's letters and at least one of John's letters. It took time for some of the others to become widely recognized in the churches — but, in the end, each of the twenty-seven books of the New Testament was reliably connected back to an eyewitness of the risen Lord or a close associate of an eyewitness of Jesus. In time, these writings became known as "the New Testament." Together with the Old Testament, they are received by Christians as the words of God himself.

Today, fragments, portions, or complete copies of more than 5,700 Greek manuscripts of the New Testament survive; differences do exist among these manuscripts, and yet the degree of agreement between them is overwhelmingly high. According to one scholar, the New Testament text is 92.6% stable, which means that all of the differences in these thousands of fragments and portions of the New Testament amount to less than 8% of the text.[1] The overwhelming majority of these differences have to do with words that are re-arranged or with differences that have no impact whatsoever on the meaning or translation of any text. Most important, not one of the differences in these manuscripts affects any essential belief that we hold about God or about his work in the world.

The New Testament is, by far, the best preserved text from the entire ancient world. Portions of the New Testament survive from the second century A.D. — less than a century after the time when God inspired eyewitnesses of the risen Lord Jesus and their close associates of eyewitnesses to write what they saw and heard.

QUESTION:

Should you have concerns about the trustworthiness of the New Testament? Why or why not?

_____

_____

_____

_____

What Do Christians Believe About the Bible?

According to the testimony of Scripture itself and declarations of faith that have been confessed for hundreds of years, the Bible is *God–breathed* and *error–free*.

"All Scripture," the Apostle Paul wrote to his protégé Timothy, "is breathed out by God and profitable for teaching, for reproof, for correction, and for training in righteousness, that the man of God may be complete, equipped for every good work." (2 Timothy 3:16–17). If Scripture is "breathed out by God," that means the words of Scripture

☑ Inspired by God
☑ Without Error
☑ Our Authority

The words of Scripture came to us from the innermost essence of God himself.

God-breathed

Scripture is:

Error-free

Our trust in the truthfulness of Scripture is rooted in our belief in the trustworthy character of God.

came to us from the innermost essence of God himself.

Moses and the prophets knew this and declared that they were writing God's own words (see, for examples, Exodus 17:14; Jeremiah 1:9; Ezekiel 1:2; Hosea 1:1). Jesus agreed with their assessment and described the words of Scripture as words from God himself (Matthew 19:4–5; Mark 12:36). This doesn't mean that God turned writers into robots, controlled from heaven through a cosmic keyboard. Instead, the biblical authors used their own free expressions, and God providentially guided their lives so that they would choose the words that conveyed his truth.

The Bible is not only *God–breathed*, however, it is also *error–free*.

"God," Paul wrote to a young pastor named Titus, "never lies" (Titus 1:2). I lie, you lie — but God never lies (Romans 3:4). With that in mind, let's ask ourselves a crucial question: if all Scripture is God–breathed and if God never lies, what does that tell us about the reliability of Scripture?

Throughout history, faithful Christians have agreed that, if God can't lie, his written revelation can't lie either. And so, our trust in the truthfulness of Scripture is rooted in our belief in the trustworthy character of God.

QUESTION:

Why can we be confident about the truthfulness of Scripture? How does the character of God influence our view of his written word?

_____

_____

_____

_____

_____

_____

A broad range of words and phrases have been used in different eras to describe the truthfulness of Scripture. One of the most important of these terms is "infallibility." The word "infallibility" comes from a Latin word that meant "unable to deceive." When we say that the Bible is "infallible," what we mean is that Scripture tells the truth and is not capable of deceiving us.

Another, more recent term that's been used to describe the truthfulness of Scripture is "inerrancy," a word that simply means "not in error."

Error-prone human beings wrote the Scriptures, but God was at work among these inspired authors and editors, preventing them from introducing any errors into his written revelation. That's why we can trust that, when all the facts are known, the Scriptures will be shown to be wholly true in everything they affirm. Inerrancy does not require Scripture to be scientifically precise, and inerrancy certainly doesn't rule out figurative language or numeric estimates in the Bible. In the words of the Chicago Statement on Biblical Inerrancy, "Scripture is inerrant, not in the sense of being absolutely precise by modern standards, but in the sense of making good its claims and achieving that measure of focused truth at which its authors aimed."

A Call to Mission

Billions of Bibles are available around the globe — but the task of translating Scripture is far from finished. Right now, more than 1,800 people groups do not have a single word of Scripture in a language that they can easily understand. What that means is that unless we translate the Scriptures into these languages, more than 180 million people will live and die without ever having heard God's Word.

Let that sink in for a moment.

More than 180 million men, women, and children.

That's six people every second for an entire year.

"The Scriptures ... are the fountains of salvation," a fourth-century church leader named Athanasius of Alexandria declared, "so that the one who thirsts may be satisfied with the living words they contain." But, for those who lack the Bible in their language, these living words remain inaccessible.

So what can you do?

You can pray.
Ask God specifically to send workers to those who have no access to the
Scriptures (Matthew 9:38).

You can give.
Find a trustworthy mission agency that translates the Scriptures;
contact the agency to find out how you can support translation efforts
around the world.

You can go.
Could God be calling you to commit your life to translate the Scriptures
for unreached people groups? My hope — my prayer — as I wrote this
chapter has been that God would use the story of how we got the Bible
to call young women and men to translate the Scriptures around the
world. Could it be that one of those people is you?

ENDNOTES

[1] K. Martin Heide, "Assessing the Stability of the Transmitted Texts of the New Testament and
The Shepherd of Hermas," The Reliability of the New Testament, ed. Robert Stewart (Minneapolis:
Fortress, 2011), 138.

These words come
from him who can make no
mistake, and who can have
no wish to deceive his
creatures. If I did not believe
in the infallibility of the Book,
I would rather be without it.
If I am to judge the Book,
it is no judge of me.

– C.H.
Spurgeon

03

The Bible

WHY USE IT?

BY MATT DAMICO

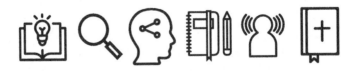

03

have you ever been in a house that lost electrical power? If so, you were probably grateful when things got fixed and you could flip on the lights again. When you don't have power, you realize how difficult it is to work and live in the dark, and how incredible it is that you usually have the power of light at your fingertips. Once you've got lights, you won't opt to work in the dark.

And yet, as Christian apologists, we occasionally end up doing just that.

When it comes to the task of spreading and defending the gospel, some questions arise: what role should the Bible play in our conversations with non–Christians? Is the Bible meant for the church and private use only, or can it play a part in our evangelism and apologetics?

Some Christians are reluctant about using the Bible in these situations, but that reluctance is unnecessary. The Bible is one of God's greatest gifts to us, "a lamp to my feet and a light to my path" (Psalm 119:105), and "no creatures is hidden from" its exposure (Hebrews 4:13). This illuminating, authoritative truth is at our fingertips, and using it in conversations with non–Christians is a way to turn the lights on, so to speak. So why would we tuck our Bibles away and work in the dark?

As Christians – "people of the book," as we're sometimes called – we should be confident about giving Scripture a role in our stand for truth. Here's why.

It's Our Final Authority

We should use the Bible because it's our highest and final authority.

What this means is that, ultimately, Christians believe what they believe not because it aligns with the rules of logic (though this is often true), nor do we hold our beliefs because they are proven by external evidence (though this is often true), nor because they're the most popular things to believe (almost never true). No, in the final analysis, we believe what we believe because the Bible says so.

It's tempting to put the Bible away and talk about things like evidence and arguments that show Christianity is true. We should be well–versed in those things, because they're often helpful and can serve to strengthen our own faith and witness. And we must be ready to respond to objections related to history, doctrine, and more. But we should not be ashamed to claim that we believe what we believe because the Bible says so.

Christians are not unique in this. Everyone – adherents to other religions and those who claim no religion at all – believes what they believe because they're committed to some final authority.

Another way to say this is that nobody is neutral. No person exists as a blank slate, devoid of desires or assumptions or hopes for the way things should be. Every person you interact with about Christianity has a lifetime's worth of experience that informs how they respond to what you say. They may claim to be objective and neutral, only interested in cold, hard facts. But nobody really is.

A great example of this comes from Tim Keller's book *Making Sense of God*. Keller relays the story of Thomas Nagel, an atheist philosopher who was honest about his inability to think about God in any kind of detached way. He said, "I want atheism to be true. It isn't just that I don't believe in God and hope that I'm right in my belief. It's that I hope there is no God! I don't want there to be a God." He's not neutral, and refreshingly honest about it.

A Muslim is committed to their holy book. An evolutionist is committed to Charles Darwin. Someone who only believes what he sees is committed to his ability to see and experience. A Christian is committed to the Bible. So don't be ashamed to say that you ultimately believe what you believe because the Bible says so.

DEFENDERS OF THE FAITH

Thomas Aquinas is one of the most influential thinkers in Christian history. His works of theology and philosophy are still widely studied, and his arguments for the existence of God, known as the "five ways" or "five proofs," remain significant. His most significant writings are *Summa Theologiae* and *Disputed Questions on Truth*.

THOMAS AQUINAS
B.1225 | D.1274

IF YOU READ ONE BOOK BY AQUINAS, MAKE IT: His "five ways" argument for the existence of God.

And be confident about actually referencing Scripture as you interact with non–Christians. This is what it means to, as the Apostle Paul says, "take every thought captive to obey Christ" (2 Corinthians 10:5). Measure the arguments of others against the Bible, and be confident about using the Bible to state your claim. Everyone will appeal to their highest authority – whether it's their logic, their senses, the Quran, or something else – so don't be ashamed to appeal to yours.

QUESTION:

1 Thessalonians 2:13 says, "And we also thank God constantly for this, that when you received the word of God, which you heard from us, you accepted it not as the word of men but as what it really is, the word of God, which is at work in you believers."

What does this verse tell us about the authority of God's Word? What makes it unique compared to other "words" or books?

_____

_____

_____

Wait...Isn't That a Problem?
One thing to be ready for is the charge of circular reasoning. It'll likely go like this:

> Christian: "Everyone who turns from sin and trusts in Jesus receives eternal life."
> Non–Christian: "How do you know that's true?"
> Christian: "Because the Bible makes that claim repeatedly."
> Non–Christian: "How do you know the Bible is true?"
> Christian: "Because the Bible claims to be God's Word, and God never lies."
> Non–Christian: "You just talked in a circle. You know the Bible is true because the Bible says it's true?"
> Christian: "You got it!"

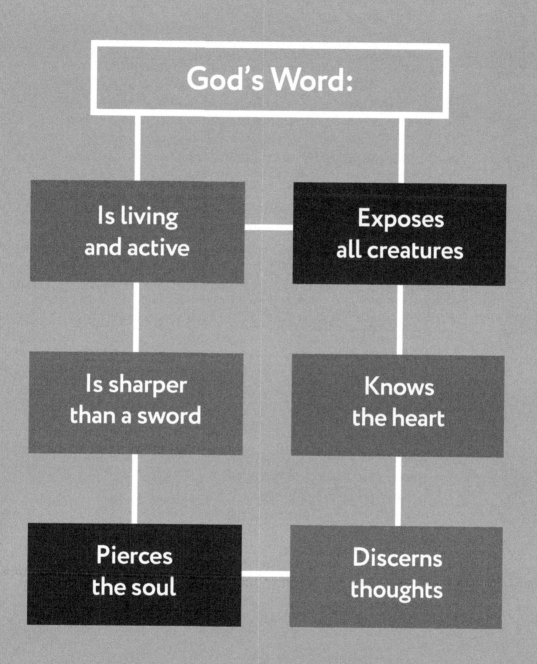

God's Word:

Is living and active

Exposes all creatures

Is sharper than a sword

Knows the heart

Pierces the soul

Discerns thoughts

Usually, circular reasoning is something to avoid. If I handed you a stick and told you it was a foot long, but you didn't believe me, how would we settle that? Probably by getting a ruler and measuring stick. We'd do that because we both agree that a ruler will tell us how many inches it is. If I say, "it's a foot long because I say it is, and you can believe me because I know how long a foot is," you would rightly laugh at me. I'd be reasoning in a circle – "trust me because I'm trustworthy!" – and it's a bad argument.

But when it comes to foundational things like our beliefs, a certain amount of circular reasoning is unavoidable. If I say, "the Bible is true because it has been proven by history and science," then history and science become the measuring stick. They become the authority, not the Bible. For us, the Bible is the highest authority, so that is where we go to establish our beliefs.

People who argue for the idea that we should only trust our senses – the things we can perceive – they have to assume the trustworthiness and accuracy of their senses. If they use something else to prove it, that other thing becomes the authority.

For Christians who believe in the authority and truthfulness of the Bible, we know something is true ultimately because the Bible says it's true. And we shouldn't be ashamed of that.

This is something many of us learned a long time ago: "Jesus loves me this I know" – how do I know it? – "for the Bible tells me so."

God's Word Is Effective

In addition to being authoritative, the Word of God has power. It can do things that we, as finite people, cannot.

Look at what the writer of Hebrews says about God's Word:

> "For the word of God is living and active, sharper than any two–edged sword, piercing to the division of soul and of spirit, of joints and of marrow, and discerning the thoughts and intentions of the heart. And no creature is hidden from his sight, but all are naked and exposed to the eyes of him to whom we must give account." (Hebrews 4:12–13)

Did you notice how he describes God's Word? It's:

- Living and active
- Sharper than a sword
- Pierces the soul

- Discerns thoughts
- Knows the heart
- Exposes all creatures

Can you do those things? Me neither.

Notice that the writer seamlessly transitions from talking about Scripture to talking about God, and there's no shift in thought. This hints at just how close the relationship is between God's Word and God himself. When Scripture speaks, God speaks, and it speaks to everyone. So Scripture can be effective for everyone. When we use God's Word, it won't return void; it is always up to something.

If the Word of God is living and active, then it's the best tool we have. When we defend and share the faith, our arguments and our evidence can be helpful. But our arguments and evidence are not living and active, sharper than any two-edged sword. So turn the lights on and work the Bible into your conversation.

I remember hearing R.C. Sproul – a great theologian and defender of the faith – share his testimony. He was a non-Christian in college when got into a conversation with someone about the Bible. The guy Sproul was talking to quoted a seemingly random Bible verse, Ecclesiastes 11:3, which says, "If a tree falls to the south or to the north, in the place where the tree falls, there it will lie." Sproul heard that verse and became a Christian. He said in jest that he's probably the only person in the history of the church to be converted through that verse, and he might be right! The story is a testament to the living power of God's Word. It's effective, so let it loose.

03

Since the Word of God is living and active, how could you use it in a conversation with a non–Christian? Imagine talking to someone about who thinks all religions worship the same God. How might you use a Bible verse like John 14:6 to interact with that person?

_____

_____

Know It

Of course, to use the Bible, you need to know it. Being a good apologist requires that you know the Bible. You don't want to get caught saying you trust the Scriptures as your highest authority, all the while neglecting to use it and know it.

Commit yourself to a life of reading, studying, memorizing, and treasuring the Bible.

Read it: To know God is to know his Word, so make a habit of reading Scripture on a daily basis. The book deepens as you know it, and it will start to change the way you think, love, and live. Attempt to master the Bible and it will master you, which is exactly what you want.

Study it: Join a Bible study. Read theology books. Read closely and pay attention to the details.

Listen to it: Be in a church where you hear the Bible preached and taught. The preached Word is one of God's means for growing us in holiness.

Memorize it: The Apostle Peter urges Christians to be ready to give a reason for the hope that's in us (1 Peter 3:15). In order to give a biblical response to challenges to the faith, we're going to need to know what the Bible says. Make a practice of memorizing Scripture. Start in Romans 8 and go from there. It'll feed your soul and enable you to articulate the faith well.

When we defend the faith, we hope not only to say that Christianity is true, we hope to compel the person we're talking with to turn to Christ. God's Word is a lamp for our feet and a light for our paths, and we want to make that way as clear as possible.

God's Word is its own
best argument.

– Vance Havner

The Bible is a window
in this prison–world
through which we may
look into eternity..

– Timothy Dwight

PART TWO

The Evidence for Christianity

04

The Uniqueness of Christ

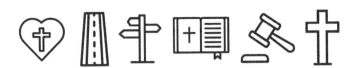

BY VINCE VITALE

GOD

Judaism

Humanism

Atheism

"No man
comes to
the Father
EXCEPT
through Me"
—Jesus

Islam

Hinduism

Buddhism

recently met a woman on the street in Chicago who told me, "I think religion is a good thing. I think all the religions are the same." Some would want to revise her comment: "I think religion is a bad thing. I think all religions are the same." Nonetheless, a lot of people are in agreement that the major religions, and even the major worldviews more generally, are fundamentally the same.

This is a common and also dangerous mistake. The more you study them, the clearer it becomes that, while the major worldviews are sometimes superficially similar, they are fundamentally very different and often at odds.

Let's take an assessment of two major worldviews according to what we care about most: love and the future. So often when I ask people what causes stress and anxiety, the answers boil down to one of these two concerns: Am I loved? What does the future hold? Christianity and Islam, two of the world's most common worldviews, have radically different things to say about what we care about most.

How Are We Loved?

The Qur'an has extremely little to say of God's love, and Al-Ghazali, arguably the most influential Muslim after Muhammad, pronounced that "[Allah] remains above the feeling of love."[1]

In the few instances where God's love is referenced in the Qur'an, it's clear that any love Allah has for human persons is reserved only for those who have *earned* it. Allah loves those who "do good" (Sura 2:195; 3:134, 148; 5:93), the "just" (5:42; 60:8) and the "even-handed" (49:9), and Allah "truly loves those who fight in solid lines for his cause" (61:4). If those are the conditions for meriting Allah's love, the list of those loved by Allah must be short.

On the crucial question of love, Islam is not only different than Christianity, but in some key respects directly opposite to it. In Islam, if you love and obey Allah, he may love you back. In Christianity, Jesus explicitly objects to only loving those who love you first: "If you love those who love you, what benefit is that to you? For even sinners love those who love them" (Luke 6:32).

In Christianity, "God shows his love for us in that while we were still sinners, Christ died for us" (Romans 5:8). While we were everything that is unlovable, God loved us enough to give his life for us. Christianity does not ask us to live good lives so that God might love us; it is because God loved us first that we are emboldened to live lives of goodness and love. On the question of love, Christianity and Islam are not just different, but the order of love is completely reversed.

One of the many people whom Allah does not like is the one who is "wasteful" (6:141; 7:31), sometimes translated as the one who is "prodigal." Jesus has something very different to say about the prodigal. In one of the most famous stories ever told, he depicts God as a loving father longing for his prodigal son to come home (Luke 15:11–32). The prodigal son has given his father every reason not to love him: demanding his inheritance early (which in that ancient culture was basically to wish his father dead), abandoning his family, wasting on wild, meaningless living what his father had worked his whole life to provide. The prodigal was proud, ungrateful, unjust, corrupt — an evildoer.

And yet at the mere sight of the prodigal son, when he is still far off in the distance, the father hikes up his long robe, exposes his legs, and takes off running (something deeply shameful for an ancient Middle Eastern man to do). He kisses his son (the text literally says that he falls on his son's neck) and embraces him and welcomes him home with the best robe (probably the father's own), a ring on his finger (probably a signet ring denoting the authority to act on behalf of the family), and sandals for his feet (a sign of freedom). What a picture of intimacy!

How are you loved? In Christianity, you are loved with the love of a running father. We are all prodigals in our own way, and Allah has no love for prodigal children. Why? Because he's not a father. In the Qur'an, Allah is not once called "father." In fact, the Qur'an says explicitly that "Allah does not beget" (112:3), thereby excluding fatherhood. In the New Testament alone, God is called "Father" over two hundred times.[2]

QUESTION:

How would you summarize the difference in the way Christianity and Islam answer the question, "Am I loved?"

_____

_____

_____

Where Are We Headed?

"All paths lead to God" is a tempting sentence. It has a certain positivity to it. But in actuality only Christianity even claims to lead to God.[3] The Christian destination is an intimate, flourishing, life–giving relationship with God himself: "This is eternal life, that they know you, the only true God, and Jesus Christ whom you have sent" (John 17:3). Primarily, for a Christian, heaven is not a place, but a person; it is not a reward, but a relationship.

The Christianization of Western culture has sometimes resulted in us projecting the destination of intimate friendship with God onto other religious worldviews. But in fact this is distinctively Christian.

In Buddhism and some traditions of Hinduism, the destination of Nirvana is the cessation of self and the elimination of desire, two essential components of personal relationship. According to tradition, it was on the very night that his son was born that Gautama Buddha left to pursue his life of detachment from anything or anyone that could cause him suffering. Contrast this with Jesus Christ, who did everything he possibly could to attach himself to our suffering in his pursuit of relationship with us.

Likewise, the destination of Islam is not relationship with Allah. The paradise spoken of in Islam is one in which Allah is almost entirely absent. Instead, paradise is depicted as a place of carnal pleasure: wine, sex, perpetual virgins, young boys who wait on men (55:56–57, 70–78; 56:34–40). Hasn't this paradise already been tried and found wanting? How many who have reached the pinnacle of earthly pleasure have testified that it is anything but paradise, that ultimately our longing for authentic relationship cannot be satisfied by anything else?

How Do We Get There?

Christianity is distinctive in its claim to lead to God. But, actually, there's a twist. If we are being precise, even Christianity doesn't claim to lead us to find God. In fact, it claims the opposite. It claims that God came to find us: "For the Son of Man came to seek and to save the lost" (Luke 19:10).

I am struck by the fact that the ideology of my cultural background was much closer to Islam than to Christianity. I accepted that "you can't rely on anyone but yourself," that "nothing is free in life," and that "you get what you deserve."

Islam affirms a similar inability to rely on anyone else for what is most important in life. If you fail to uphold the mandatory Pillars of Islam, no one can save you. In the words of the Qur'an, "We have bound each human being's destiny to his neck" (17:13), and "that man will only have what he has worked toward" (53:38–39).

Buddhism and Hinduism are in agreement in so far as it is only through the personal effort of pursuing the four noble truths or following the noble eightfold path or meriting good karma — in other words, it is only on the basis of what you do — that one attains the goal of enlightenment.

DEFENDERS OF THE FAITH

G.K. CHESTERTON
B.1874 | D.1936

G.K. Chesterton was a prolific writer, producing books, poems, short stories, essays, and more over the course of his career. C.S. Lewis referred to Chesterton's book, *The Everlasting Man*, as "the best popular apologetic I know." His wit was sharp, and he had the uncanny ability to present the truth in surprising and illuminating ways. His influence as an apologist was considerable in his day, and continues in the number of prominent Christian thinkers who cite Chesterton as an influence.

IF YOU READ ONE BOOK BY CHESTERTON, MAKE IT: *Orthodoxy*

Four truths about Christianity:

God shows his love for us in
that while we were still sinners,
Christ died for us.

God does not deal with us according
to our sins, nor repay us according
to our iniquities.

There is a promise of salvation
for those who trust Jesus.

Jesus conceived of our eternal home,
he purchased it, he is preparing it,
and one day he will move us into it.

Here again, Jesus stands alone. He urges us, "Come to me, all who labor and are heavy laden, and I will give you rest. Take my yoke upon you, and learn from me, for I am gentle and lowly in heart, and you will find rest for your souls. For my yoke is easy, and my burden is light" (Matthew 11:28–30). Jesus explicitly offers to bear our burdens for us: "'He himself bore our sins in his body on the tree" (1 Peter 2:24).

Salvation is therefore not something we earn, but a "free gift" (Romans 6:23): "by grace you have been saved through faith. And this is not your own doing; it is the gift of God, not a result of works, so that no one may boast" (Ephesians 2:8–9). Contrary to every other major belief system, the Christian God "does not deal with us according to our sins, nor repay us according to our iniquities" (Psalm 103:10). So great is his love.

Because where we are headed in Christianity is based on what God has already done and not on what we might do, we can be assured of our destiny in a way that is not possible in Islam. No one can know in Islam if he has done enough. Even if the scales tip in his favor on the last day, Allah's sovereignty is such that he is not bound by the scales. For even those who obey Allah, "the punishment of their Lord is not something to feel safe from" (70:28). The Qur'an instructs even Muhammad to say, "I do not know what will be done with me or you" (46:9).

In Christianity, there is a promise of salvation for those who trust Jesus. Explaining his motivation for writing, one of the biblical authors says, "I write these things to you who believe in the name of the Son of God, that you may know that you have eternal life" (1 John 5:13). Likewise, Paul says, "If you confess with your mouth that Jesus is Lord and believe in your heart that God raised him from the dead, you will be saved" (Romans 10:9). Many other verses could be cited in support. Jesus Christ's starting point is everyone else's finish line — the assurance of salvation!

A Muslim taxi driver once told me, "I'm terrified of judgment. Any Muslim will tell you that." After I explained that in Christianity we don't need to fear judgment because Jesus bore our judgment, he responded, with heavy emotion on his face, "It's a beautiful story. I wish it were true."

In Christianity, Jesus conceived of our eternal home, he purchased it, he is preparing it, and one day he will move us into it. He is the architect, the buyer, the decorator, and the moving company. This could not be further from having to put a roof over our own heads. This is getting so much more than we have striven for or could ever deserve.

So to return to our question, do all paths lead to God? No. None do. Some claim to lead us to some sort of reward or enlightenment. Naturalistic worldviews must admit that ultimately we are headed nowhere — for personal death and species extinction. Even Christianity claims not that we are led to God but that God's love led him to us.

When it comes to what keeps us up at night — Am I loved? What does my future hold? — we are faced with a choice between very different ways of viewing the world. Must we fight to earn love or are we free to enjoy it? Must others fight to earn our love or will we share it freely? Is our future uncertain or is it secure? And will it include the relationship we long for most?

In Jesus and in Jesus alone, because of who he is, what he taught, and the sacrifice he made, we find true freedom, unconditional love, total security, and everlasting relationship. That is the unique and wonderful offer that the God of the Bible makes to you.

This chapter was adapted from *Jesus Among Secular Gods* by Ravi Zacharias and Vince Vitale (FaithWords 2017).

QUESTION:

Christianity offers an assurance of salvation that is unique among religions. What's the basis of this confidence that Christians can enjoy? How might you incorporate this unique feature of Christianity into your next evangelistic or apologetic conversation?

_____

_____

_____

_____

_____

ENDNOTES

[1] Al–Ghazali, *Al–Ghazali on the Ninety–Nine Beautiful Names of God* (Islamic Texts Society, 1999).

[2] See Robert H. Stein, "Fatherhood of God," Biblestudytools.com, http://www.bible–studytools.com/dictionaries/bakers–evangelical–dictionary/fatherhood–of–god.html. Accessed 12 Sept. 2016.

[3] I am indebted to my colleagues Andy Bannister and Tanya Walker, whom I first heard make this point. For Tanya's discussion of it, see her chapter "But...What About Other Religions?" in *A New Kind of Apologist*, edited by Sean McDowell (Eugene, OR: Harvest House Publishers, 2016). For Andy's discussion, see Chapter 3 of his *The Atheist Who Didn't Exist* (Oxford: Monarch Books, 2015).

Apply the tests of truth to the person and the message of Jesus Christ. You see not only his exclusivity, but also his uniqueness.

– Ravi Zacharias

05

Creation's Witness to God

BY DAN DEWITT

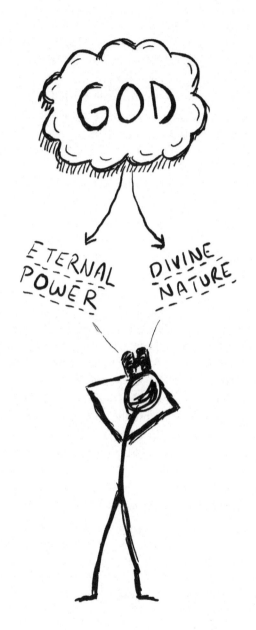

t he world is filled with wonder. The world is filled with horror. We live in a wonderful, horrible place.

The Bible says that as God made creation he called it good (Genesis 1:10). When he was finished, God said it was all good (Genesis 1:31). We are amazed at the goodness of God's creation all the time: when we walk through the forest in the fall, when we stand on a beach looking at the ocean, or when we stare at the stars filling the night sky. This is what makes the world wonderful.

Don't Ignore the Expiration Date

But creation isn't all good anymore. It's spoiled. Have you ever taken a drink of spoiled milk? You probably spit it out right away. Milk is good, but if it goes bad it will turn your stomach to drink it. The world is a little like that. It used to be perfect. But something has gone terribly wrong. As C.S. Lewis once said, "Nature has all the air of a good thing spoiled."

That's because the Bible says that something has gone terribly wrong. God created and placed Adam and Eve in the Garden of Eden as his representatives. They were made in God's image so that all of creation could see something of what God was like. The world God made revealed his glory.

But then the unthinkable happened. Adam and Eve chose not to fulfill their God–given design as God's image bearers. They chose not to reflect God's goodness. They chose to decide for themselves what was right and what was wrong. They suppressed or denied the knowledge of God. As a result, a curse came over the first couple and the world in which they lived (Genesis 3).

This is what makes the world horrible. We live in this kind of weird mixture of wonder and horror. But it all still points to the creator. Creation, though under a curse, still points to God. Humanity – me and you, and everyone else – still carries the image of the creator. Creation points to the creator through a curse.

05

Invisible Attributes

The Apostle Paul explains that there are a couple of specific ways the world points to God. In the book of Romans, Paul says:

> For what can be known about God is plain to them, because God has shown it to them. For his *invisible attributes*, namely, his *eternal power* and his *divine nature*, have been clearly perceived, ever since the creation of the world, in the things that have been made. So they are without excuse. (Romans 1:19–20)

Paul explains that God's invisible attributes, his eternal power and his divine nature, are on full display in creation. Just by looking at the world we can see that it must have come from something — or someone — really powerful. The chance that our massive universe could allow for one planet to host intelligent life (people like you who can read books like this) is absolutely breathtaking. Where could such a world have come from?

The Apostle Paul shows us that this is one of the ways God revealed himself: by creating the world in such a way that is really hard to deny that it came from an all–powerful being. That, of course, doesn't mean people don't try to deny it. But deep down they know there is a God.

To deny an all–powerful source behind creation, Paul explains, people must suppress the knowledge of God that is staring them in the face when they look into the heavens. King David spoke of this when he wrote, "The heavens declare the glory of God" (Psalm 19). Creation gives us a witness of this invisible attribute of God, his eternal power. We can suppress it, but we cannot ignore it. It is all around us.

QUESTION:

How would you answer the question, "Why should creation lead me to conclude that God exists?" How could Psalm 19:1–6 help inform your answer? What specific parts of creation would you list as evidence of God's power?

_____

_____

_____

_____

The Beginning

One of the ways to get around this, for people who don't want to believe in God, is to deny that the universe had a beginning. A lot of people have done this throughout human history. Even the brilliant scientist Albert Einstein taught the world was eternal.

In time, Einstein changed his mind, largely because his own theory pointed this direction. Other scientific discoveries have provided evidence that the world had a beginning, too, like the ability to see planets moving away from us through the Hubble Telescope. Or, for another example, the presence of what is called cosmic background radiation, evidence of an explosive creation event, all over the universe.

So, it's no longer cool for scientists to believe the universe is eternal. But if the world did have a beginning, then people who want to suppress the knowledge of God have to come up with some alternative explanation for where the world came from.

One option is the world came from nothing. However, since most people don't find it convincing that something could come from nothing, others have developed a theory called *multiverse*.

Even the famous scientist/celebrity Neil deGrasse Tyson teaches that it is possible that there are tons of universes (multiverse) outside of our universe. Keep in mind that we cannot see, let alone study, anything beyond our universe. But that doesn't keep people from supposing there might be billions and billions of universes beyond our own. Imagine if these universes gave birth to new universes and the number of universes kept growing. At some point a universe might plop into existence that could allow for a planet like ours that can host intelligent life forms (people like you who are still reading this book). Problem solved!

All of this demonstrates that if you want to suppress the knowledge of God and his power, it seems like you don't need much, if any, physical evidence. Just come up with any far-fetched idea, get a few scientists to nod their heads in approval, and you're good to go. Maybe that's why some scientists go so far as to suggest that we came from aliens. That's a theory known as *panspermia*, but we don't have time to talk about crazy alien nonsense right now.

Nature reveals God's power and his character.

Five truths about creation's witness to God:

The moral law points to a moral lawgiver.

To be made right with God we must know to Gospel, the story of Jesus, found in Scripture.

God has written his law on our hearts.

What we can see about God in creation is enough to condemn us for rejecting God.

But, wait a minute, you might think, do we have any evidence for a powerful source creating our world? Yep. We do. What is it? The answer: the universe.

Robert Jastrow, a scientist for NASA, who never professed his own belief in God, said that the universe itself is proof that there is something outside of nature. So, if there is something outside of nature, it isn't a stretch of logic to say it is something supernatural. The fact that the natural world exists, that it had a beginning, points to some really powerful source outside of nature — something supernatural — that brought it into being. That powerful source is God.

The Moral of the Story

There's more. Paul said that nature reveals two things: God's power and his character. Thus far we've only talked about God's power. Paul also says that God has made the world in such a way that we can learn something about God's "divine nature."

But how does creation allow us to see into God's character or his nature? It's likely not the same way that we see God's power. After all, there could be an evil all-powerful being capable of making stuff, kind of like an evil genie in a bottle. How does Paul think we will learn of God's divine nature from creation?

Paul says that God has written his law on our hearts (Romans 2:15). That means that to be human is to know — deep down — basic matters of right and wrong. That's why we all, Christian and non-Christian alike, regularly say things like, "That's wrong! That's unfair! That's un-just!" Such statements demonstrate that in our hearts we know there is a moral order to the universe.

The moral law points to a moral lawgiver. Think about it this way: if there is a lawgiver, then we should expect there to be a moral law. If there isn't a moral lawgiver then we shouldn't expect there to be a moral law. So, what kind of world do we live in, one with or without a moral law?

We live in a world governed by moral laws. So, what does that mean? It means there is a moral lawgiver.

What I don't mean to say is that the moral law is like speed limits you see posted on the highway. Things like speed limits are man-made regulations to keep people from driving like morons and killing each other. We don't need God for speed limits.

But we do need a moral law to know that killing each other is wrong and to obligate others to this law, to expect them to see it as their moral duty not to kill. That's what I'm getting at. We all have a deep sense that some things are right (like helping each other) and some things are wrong (like killing each other) hardwired into us.

Where does this moral sense come from? It comes from a lawgiver. It comes from God.

People who want to suppress the knowledge of God have to come up with a way to explain our moral sense of duty and obligation apart from God. This is often referred to as *secularism*, an attempt to understand the world without having to bring "religion" into things. But trying to get a moral law without a moral lawgiver is really difficult. Actually, it's impossible.

One famous professor from Canada who taught ethics at the University of Calgary, a guy named Kai Nielson, admits this much. As an atheist he would like to find a way to have a moral law without a moral lawgiver. But he recognizes that he can't. He says that reason cannot lead us to a moral point of view.

So where does our moral point of view come from? The Apostle Paul explains that it comes from God. God has created the world in such a way that his eternal power and his divine nature are clearly seen just by being human and living in God's world. People who don't want to acknowledge God have to suppress this knowledge and try to come up with other explanations.

DEFENDERS OF THE FAITH

C.S. LEWIS
B.1898 | D.1963

C.S. Lewis is best known for his Chronicles of Narnia series, but his literary gifts gave expression to some of the most accessible and influential apologetic writings of the 20th century. Lewis dealt with his own doubts and objections to Christianity as a young man, eventually converting to Christianity in his 30s. He spent much of his career explaining and defending the Christian faith, and a number of his books continue to be read, like *The Screwtape Letters*, *The Problem of Pain*, *Surprised by Joy*, and many more.

IF YOU READ ONE BOOK BY LEWIS, MAKE IT: *Mere Christianity*

05

How would you summarize this moral argument for God to someone? What are some examples of laws or values that are shared by everyone, and what does this reveal about humanity?

_____

_____

_____

_____

No Excuses

So, why doesn't everyone just believe that there is a powerful and moral source behind the universe? Shouldn't God's invisible attributes lead any thinking person to believe in him? Nope.

That's because people don't want a moral lawgiver. Like Adam and Eve, we prefer to decide for ourselves what is good and not good. We exchange the glory of God in creation for lesser things. We'd rather worship idols than worship God. We need God to open our eyes.

Paul says that when people reject the creator, God gives them over to their own desires. To quote C.S. Lewis again, "There are only two kinds of people in the end: those who say to God, 'Thy will be done,' and those to whom God says, in the end, 'Thy will be done.'" If people want to deny the powerful and moral source behind creation, God will let them.

But because God has revealed himself in creation, Paul says people who suppress the knowledge of God are without excuse (Romans 1:20). That means that what we can see about God in creation is enough to condemn us for rejecting God. But to be made right with God, we need more than simply to see God in nature. We must know the gospel, the story of Jesus, found in Scripture.

Nature can point us only so far. The gospel alone can take us home.

The world is like
a curious piece of
tapestry, in which we
may see the skill and
wisdom of him
that made it.

– Thomas
Watson

06

Jesus,
Easter,
and You

BY DAN DARLING

06

Who is Jesus? The answer to this question is the foundation of Christianity. His deity is enshrined in all three major Christian creeds and has been held by the church for its two thousand years of history.[1]

Every generation faces new temptations to diminish or doubt the deity of Jesus. Even those who claim to be true believers have trouble grasping who Jesus is. It's less hassle for us to just place Jesus where we want to, in a long line of inspirational religious figures. But for the Christian story to work at all, Jesus has to be more than a first–century Gandhi–like figure.

My aim in this chapter is not only to fill your head with more information, but to see God by his grace penetrate your heart with the truth of his Word.

I hope to show why Jesus is less compelling as a mere guru than he is as the Son of God, the Savior of the world.

Easter's Big "If"

As much as the Christian narrative seems to offer answers, it mostly asks questions. Perhaps the biggest question it asks is the one we celebrate on the most important Christian holiday, Easter. Underneath all the yellow bunnies, jelly beans, and fake grass, Easter asks a question: "What if this really happened like the Bible says it did?"

What is the thing the Bible says happened on Easter? It makes the claim that Jesus died on a cross — literally died and was buried in a rich man's tomb. Three days later he broke off the chains of death, and forty days after that he ascended back to heaven as the reigning king of the universe.

Believe it or not, in this chapter I'm not going to ask you to accept that the resurrection event really happened, though I think the evidence of Jesus' bodily resurrection is compelling. I want to ask and answer the question, "What if Jesus was more than a guru, a wonderful teacher, or an inspirational figure?"

Because if what we claim on Easter happened, it changes everything about you, me, and the world in which we live. I hope you'll be so compelled by the story you'll want to believe it's true. Here are three reasons why, if Jesus is more than a guru, his life changes everything.

Reason #1: If Easter is true, we finally have someone we can trust. If Jesus really did rise from the dead, he is someone we can trust. The Gospels record Jesus promising to do what he said he would do — rise from the dead. Listen to Jesus' words recorded in John's Gospel:

> So the Jews said to him, "What sign do you show us for doing these things?" Jesus answered them, "Destroy this temple, and in three days I will raise it up." The Jews then said, "It has taken forty-six years to build this temple, and will you raise it up in three days?" But he was speaking about the temple of his body. When therefore he was raised from the dead, his disciples remembered that he had said this, and they believed the Scripture and the word that Jesus had spoken. (John 2:18–22)

Jesus didn't simply predict his own death and resurrection, but said that he would raise himself:

> For this reason the Father loves me, because I lay down my life that I may take it up again. (John 10:17)

Throughout history, many have claimed to have risen from the dead. Every generation has folks who claim to have come back from heaven or hell. Most of these accounts can't hold up to the tiniest scrutiny, not the scrutiny Jesus' claims have withstood.

If Jesus rose from the dead as the Scriptures say, it not only means he is someone you can trust, but it signifies that Jesus is someone you must listen to, for he is the power of God.

If Easter is true, it not only proves Jesus' trustworthiness when it comes to his own words, but it proves God's faithfulness to keep promises to his people throughout history. The Old Testament prophets and writers of Scripture predicted a Messiah who would come near to us as both man and God, right down to the most specific of details, such as the exact town where Jesus would be born, the circumstances around his birth, and the reaction among political leaders. According to Jewish scholar Alfred Eidersheim, there are around 456 specific passages that refer to Jesus the Messiah in the Old Testament.

Every generation longs for leaders it can trust, and ours is no different. Our expectations for leadership are why we hold our pastors, politicians, and business leaders up to such high and impossible standards. Nobody, not even the best and brightest, makes the cut. Every single leader disappoints.

But according to the Christian story, there is one who promised to

QUESTION:

How does the resurrection of Christ make him uniquely trustworthy? Would he be trustworthy if he hadn't risen from the dead, especially in light of verses like Mark 8:31 and Luke 9:22?

_____

_____

_____

_____

_____

Reason #2: If Easter is true, then we too will rise again.
If Easter is true, Jesus not only has the power to raise himself from death, but also to raise his people from death. Listen to the words of the Apostle Paul, who once was a skeptic:

> But in fact Christ has been raised from the dead, the firstfruits of those who have fallen asleep. For as by a man came death, by a man has come also the resurrection of the dead. For as in Adam all die, so also in Christ shall all be made alive. (1 Corinthians 15:20–22)

The Christian story makes the claim that if Jesus rose from the dead, those he redeems will rise again.

Death is not the final answer. Death has been defeated. Jesus asserted his eternal, life–giving power at the funeral of one of his best friends, Lazarus:

> Jesus said to her, "I am the resurrection and the life. Whoever believes in me, though he die, yet shall he live, and everyone who lives and believes in me shall never die. Do you believe this?" (John 11:25–26)

And again at another gathering he proclaimed:

> For as the Father raises the dead and gives them life, so also the Son gives life to whom he will. (John 5:21)

Jesus' claims are otherworldly. This is more than a go–to–heaven–and–back experience. In the above passages, Jesus is professing to be more than a guru or inspirational figure, but one who holds our very lives in his all–powerful and capable hands.

This is the one power we wish we had. Here we sit in the twenty–first century at the apex of human progress, and yet we are as close to solving the problem of death as cavemen.

A few years ago, I walked the halls of Children's Memorial Hospital. My daughter Emma, three at the time, had contracted a strange virus that

What if this really happened the way the Bible says it did?

left her entire body swollen and disfigured. We were in arguably the best children's hospital in Chicago, at the cutting edge of medical science, and yet the doctors were mystified as to the nature of her illness. Emma pulled through and her health was restored, but in that same hospital were less fortunate parents whose children clutched the last fragments of life, their bodies wracked by cancer or other fatal diseases.

Death is why we have hospitals. We walk through the doors hoping beyond hope for healing cures. Yet even as the most brilliant minds apply their genius to the human condition, death visits with its spotless record. Everyone dies.

But if what Jesus says about himself is true, it means there is hope beyond the grave. It means the Christian narrative is more than a feel-good story; it actually holds the answers to life.

In Christ, death is not the final word:

QUESTION:

Humanity always looks for ways to avoid or delay death, and yet everyone deserves it because their sin separates them from God. How does the life and ministry of Jesus address both of those realities? (Read: Hebrews 2:14–15 and Revelation 21:4)

_____
_____
_____
_____
_____

DEFENDERS OF THE FAITH

Francis Schaeffer was a philosopher and apologist who had a prolific career as a writer and speaker. He and his wife opened a home in Switzerland, called "L'Abri," where they hosted guests to discuss matters of philosophy and faith. He wrote more than 20 books, including apologetic classics like *He Is There* and *He Is Not Silent*. Though he died more than three decades ago, a number of active apologists cite Schaeffer as an important influence.

FRANCIS SCHAEFFER
B.1912 | D.1984

IF YOU READ ONE BOOK BY SCHAEFFER, MAKE IT: *The God Who Is There*

When the perishable puts on the imperishable, and the mortal puts on immortality, then shall come to pass the saying that is written: "Death is swallowed up in victory." "O death, where is your victory? O death, where is your sting?" The sting of death is sin, and the power of sin is the law. But thanks be to God, who gives us the victory through our Lord Jesus Christ. (1 Corinthians 15:54–57)

We are forced to admit our powerlessness against the cycle of death. Medicine, technology, and financial investment only get us so far. But if Easter is true, everything changes.

Reason #3: If Easter is true, we can actually know God.

This is the last and most audacious claim Jesus makes. If he really died and rose again and is alive today, God is more than an esoteric, ethereal concept. God came near and can be known.

The Christian story says we were made to live in community with God. It says human beings were originally created to reflect God's image and to walk in communion with him. But sin, the choice to become our own little gods, shattered the creator's original intent. From Eden, we've been alienated from the God who sculpted us with his hands. But there is good news.

**Three reasons why
Easter changes everything:**

If Easter is true	we finally have someone we can trust.
If Easter is true	then we too will rise again.
If Easter is true	we can actually know God.

Jesus' life and death closed that gap. He is the atonement for sin and his resurrection is proof that the Father was satisfied. Through Christ we can know God personally. The gospel says two equally true things. First, we have sinned and violated God's holiness and can't possibly atone for our sin. And second, that God loved us so much that he, in Christ, suffered the punishment for that sin and offers us new life in Jesus. This is the uniqueness of the Christian story. It doesn't present a God who wants us to try hard to please him. It presents a God who did the work to reach us through Christ. If what Jesus claimed is true, and if Jesus was raised from the dead, this reality changes everything.

Jesus offers an *exclusive* path, but an *inclusive* offer — one way to God offered to all who believe. And how could it be any different? Is there another who fits the description of Jesus, who meets the qualifications?

If Jesus' story is true, you and I are faced with a choice. We can either bow before Jesus as God and Lord, or we can arch our backs and reject him. We can choose life or we can choose death. We can choose the hope of that future city that God is making for his own, or we can choose hell.

> **God loved us so much that he, in Christ, suffered the punishment for that sin and offers us new life in Jesus.**

06

More Than a Guru

I hope you see by now that the Jesus we need has to be more than a mere guru, an inspirational figure whose words and rhetoric lift us to greater heights. Jesus has to be more than that or he is none of that.

We need a victorious king, a sacrificial lamb of God, a Savior, a Lord, a creator. Gurus rise and fall. Inspirational figures die. Powerful and benevolent leaders, even at their best, cannot restore and renew the fallen cosmos, nor can they close the gap between man and God. Only Jesus the God–man can do this.

The real Jesus, the Jesus of Scripture, is compelling. The only logical response is to bow the knee and worship him as Lord and king.

This material was adapted from *The Original Jesus: Trading the Myths We Create for the Savior Who Is* by Daniel Darling (Baker Books, 2015).

ENDNOTES

[1] For a helpful summary of the early church's position on Jesus's deity, check out this piece by Nathan Busenitz, "Did the Early Church Affirm Jesus' Deity?," *The Cripplegate*, accessed May 24, 2014, http://thecripplegate.com/did-the-early-church-affirm-jesus-deity/.

[2] Alfred Edersheim, *The Life and Times of Jesus the Messiah* (Longmans, Green, 1883), 163. Two helpful lay-level resources are Lee Strobel's The Case for Christ (Grand Rapids: Zondervan, 2001) and *The Case for the Real Jesus* (Grand Rapids: Zondervan, 2007).

If in Christ we have hope in this life only, we are of all people most to be pitied. But in fact Christ has been raised from the dead, the firstfruits of those who have fallen asleep.

– 1 Corinthians 15:19–20

PART THREE

The Threats to Christianity

07

The Problem of Evil

BY TREY BRUNSON

e vil is one of those words you almost don't have to define. We all see it. We all feel it. When you hear names like Hitler, Bin Laden, Manson, and Dahmer you cringe a bit thinking of how real and present evil is. In our culture, war, sex–trafficking, slavery, terrorism, and violence on a massive scale are sadly all too common. The existence of this kind of evil poses a serious threat to Christianity.

Our world and our lives are riddled with evil, pain, and suffering. All of us struggle through much of life and are regularly overwhelmed by what we see around us. That's why so many have said that the problem of evil is the greatest theological problem and potentially the greatest threat to Christianity.

What's the Problem?

So, what exactly do we mean by "the problem of evil?" The Greek philosopher Epicurus originated the argument when he asked, "Is God willing to prevent evil, but not able? Then he is not omnipotent. Is he able, but not willing? Then he is malevolent. Is he both able and willing? Then whence cometh evil? Is he neither able nor willing? Then why call him God?"[1]

The problem of evil revolves around three biblical claims about God:

The Scriptures teach that:
- God is all–powerful (Nehemiah 9:6; Psalm 33:9; Isaiah 44:24; Romans 1:20; Colossians 1:6–7)
- God is all–good (Psalm 100:5; Psalm 145:17; Nahum 1:7; Mark 10:18; John 3:16)
- God is all–wise (Job 12:13; Proverbs 2:6–7; Daniel 2:20; Romans 16:27; James 1:5).

If those things are true, then why is there evil? The presence of evil has to challenge one of these claims. It doesn't deny the existence of God formally, but it does functionally.

Maybe the most appropriate way to state the problem is in the way we most commonly express it, "Why, God?" You see, the problem of evil isn't just a logical question that needs to be rationally answered, it's also an emotional challenge that crowds God out of our hearts as much as our minds when we hurt.

07

How We Should Think About Evil

Let's start with the logical problem. We have this impasse: a God who claims to be powerful, good, and wise. And yet, inside his creation, there exists rampant evil. How do these fit together? Is there a way to resolve the tension?

There have been several answers posed, but we have to be content with the fact that, while there are some answers to the challenge of a sovereign God who allows evil, there will never be a fully satisfying answer logically or emotionally for the experience of evil and suffering in our lives.

The Reality of Evil

The Bible is very clear on the presence and problem of evil. Some religions and several cults attempt to deal with the problem of evil by saying evil doesn't exist, that suffering is merely an illusion. The Bible makes no such claims. The Bible sees sin, evil, and suffering as not only realities but as enemies under the sovereign control of God.

From the beginning, immediately after the fall of Genesis 3, God promised that evil was on a time clock and will be dealt with in God's timing. Since the fall, the Lord has consistently taken the side of those who are marginalized and weak in the Scriptures (Deuteronomy 10:17–18; Deuteronomy 27:19; Zechariah 7:9–10). The Lord always defends the weak and eventually exercises judgment on the wicked.

Could God eradicate all evil in the world immediately? Absolutely, but that would mean destroying all of us because we are all fallen and sinners (Romans 3:10–12; Romans 3:23; Romans 14:1–3; Psalms 53:1–3; Isaiah 53:6). God has chosen to allow evil to exist in order to show his glory, power, and love.

In fact, we see in Scripture that God is able to take painful and evil events and use them for good (Genesis 50:20; Proverbs 16:4; Romans 8:28). The point being that, unlike so many religions and philosophies, the Bible is clear that evil is real, that it has a purpose, and that God is in control despite what we feel.

The Work of Jesus

There is a problem of evil, but only from our experience, not from God's perspective. Everything is happening just as he planned, proving him worthy of glory, honor, and power (Revelation 4:11). God has not yet eradicated evil, but he has dealt it its final blow through the work of Jesus.

The Bible says that God got involved in our suffering by sending Jesus. The Son of God stepped out of eternity to live as a human and to die as a divine sacrifice. His death had nothing to do with his sins (since he was sinless) and in fact, we are told that our sins were placed on him. He suffered in our place so that God could forgive and redeem his creation.

In the greatest act of evil in the history of the world, Jesus was killed. God the Father accepted his sacrifice and three days later Jesus rose from the grave, ascending to heaven where he sits enthroned.

Jesus has in fact dealt with evil in that greatest act of evil. The Scriptures tell us that while Christ has redeemed his people, God is being gracious to allow more time for more people to hear what Christ has done for them before he ends evil in an ultimate act of justice (2 Peter 3:8–10).

The metanarrative of the Scriptures is that God is not taking us back to Eden but to a New Creation, one where there is no sin, suffering, evil, or potential for them ever again. The Bible sees the completed work of Christ not being solely his death, resurrection, and ascension but also his return, reign, and re–creating of all things (Ephesians 1:7–10).

The work of Jesus is not only God's answer to the problem of evil, it is our only hope and help as those who are evil and do evil things.

QUESTION:

How would you summarize the problem of evil? How does the death and resurrection of Jesus address that problem?

_____

_____

_____

_____

Tension Exists

So, the Bible is not silent when it comes to the logical problem of evil. God has a purpose, one that we see is producing something bigger than any of us can imagine. Evil has a timeframe, one where it is allowed to exist because it is part of a greater good and a better story. This may leave us with tension and questions, but the Bible is okay with that.

As Tim Keller said, "Just because you can't see or imagine a good reason why God might allow something to happen doesn't mean there can't be one." God has a reason and a plan, and we have to trust him. While the Bible gives us some substance to lean on, it also leaves us with a lot of room to question, cry out, and pray. It's impossible to know the mind of God and to understand the bigger picture when we are only a small part in God's great story. We can rest in the fact that God is sovereign, he loves us, and that in time all things will become clear (1 Corinthians 13:12).

How Should We Feel About Evil?

The Bible doesn't just tell us how to think about these things, it also helps us know how to feel when we experience suffering and evil. One prime source for this guidance is the book of Job. Job operates as a salve for those who are hurting and struggling with the problem of evil. It's the story of a man who deals with natural evil and moral evil on a level few of us can comprehend.

In Job, while we learn a lot about life, suffering, and God, there are few logically satisfying answers for the problem of evil. Yet, Job's book is given to those who suffer to help them suffer well.

Let's consider Job.

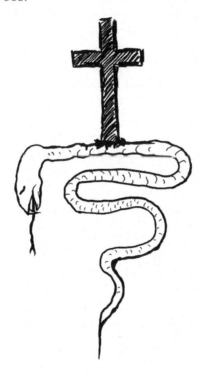

There Are Things Above Us We Don't Know

The opening chapter of Job gives us one of the most interesting scenes in all of the Bible. In Heaven, God is on the throne and somehow, Satan enters the scene. God allows Satan to test Job through suffering. There is so much about this scene that is puzzling. The point that we're supposed to take away is that there are things above us that we won't understand on this side of heaven. Job teaches us that there is a reason for seemingly senseless suffering, but it may be above us.

There Are Things Around Us We Don't Understand

As Satan exits the heavenly court in Job 1, the suffering begins. Job 1:13–2:10 is hard to read. It's hard to read because it feels like real life in a painful way. There are four reports, two of natural evil (evil that results not from human beings but from nature as a result of the fall), and two from moral evil (evil that results from human activity). On top of that, there is Job's personal suffering in his body, mind, and spirit. It's a comprehensive glimpse of evil in the experience of one man.

There are things that happen around us in our lives that we have no way of understanding. As Job got report after report, the confusion, bewilderment, and anguish sank deeper and deeper. One tragedy is perplexing enough, but suffering on this scale is incomprehensible. Job teaches that there is a reason, but our experience in this life may be beyond comprehension.

There Are Things in Us We Can't Process

Job 3–37 can be difficult reading. Job's friends initially rally around their hurting friend. Yet, as we read and hear from Job's friends, we hear some interesting comments. You see, in the mind of Job's friends, there is no explanation for suffering on this level apart from God's judgment on Job for some sin. They don't have the vantage point that we have as readers. They haven't seen what's above.

Job's suffering isn't a consequence of his sin, it's the result of living in a fallen world. But his friends don't know that and can't see that. Job teaches us that there is a reason, but we often can't process what's happening inside our own sinful hearts.

Four truths about suffering from Job:

01 There are things above us we don't know.

03 There are things in us we can't process.

02 There are things around us we don't understand.

04 There are things ahead of us we can't comprehend.

There Are Things Ahead of Us We Can't Comprehend

Outside of the initial chapters of Job, we don't hear from God until chapters 38–41. When God begins to speak, everything else goes silent. Then in Job 42 we read something that felt impossible in Job 3: that God had a plan for Job's good.

In Job 42, the Lord restores, blesses, and brings beauty from ashes (Isaiah 61:3). Suffering is deafening. Pain is blinding. Evil is overwhelming. Yet, God has a future for his children that is greater than we could ever begin to imagine. Job teaches us that there is a reason, but we can't even begin to imagine what it is or how great things ahead of us could be.

QUESTION:

Read Deuteronomy 29:29 and Isaiah 55:8–9. How can these verses influence the way we think about the problem of evil?

_____

_____

_____

_____

_____

_____

Trust God

The point of the book of Job is that we cannot trust what we feel or see, but we can trust God. While unbearable pain defined Job's life, God was there and in control.

One takeaway from the book of Job is that our suffering will always be a mystery to us, but there is comfort in knowing that God is always in control and always accomplishing something through our suffering. We have to trust God because, despite our questions, our pain, and our confusion, evil is not a problem for him. We can trust God because he is all powerful, all good, and all wise. We can trust God, even when we hurt.

Do not fear the shadowy places. You will never be the first one there. Another went ahead and down until he came out the other side.

– N.D. Wilson

"I'm Spiritual, but Not Religious"

BY RANDALL BRELAND

08

f you are keeping up with the reboot of the *Star Wars* franchise, one of the fan-favorite characters is Chirrut Îmwe, the blind monk in *Rogue One*. Despite his blindness, he is deeply spiritual and in tune with "the force." During a battle against Empire soldiers, Chirrut chants, "The force is with me. I'm one with the force. The force is with me. I'm one with the force." By chanting, he channels courage, steps into the fight, and defeats a dozen or so soldiers. The scene is both mesmerizing and a reasonably accurate depiction of 21st-century American spirituality.

The growth of American spirituality as a substitute for the Christian faith is rapid. More and more people are rejecting the truths about God and Jesus presented by the Bible and are replacing them with an undefined, vague spirituality. Many who embrace this new spiritualism argue that they are "spiritual" people but "not religious."

This American spirituality is growing most quickly in the youngest generations. Among younger millennials (those born between 1990 and 1996), 36% identify as religiously unaffiliated. Generation Z is a moniker given to those born between 1995 and 2010.[1] While 78% of this youngest generation believes in God or a higher power, only half attend religious services on a regular basis, and a mere 8% cite a religious leader as a role model.[2] These stats point to one haunting truth: "the younger the generation, the more post-Christian it is."[3] They are interested in spiritual things but flee from religious matters.

Four Observations About American Spirituality
How do we engage the spiritual-but-not-religious? Let's begin with four observations about this growing American spirituality.

Observation 1: Young Americans Are Unfamiliar with Christianity
Most young Americans do not know the basic stories of the Bible or the essential beliefs of Christianity. Americans today find attending church to hold little value and are just not interested in it. If you grew up in a family that regularly attended church and you or your parents have regularly read the Bible, your experience is not normal.

In fact, a negative view of Christians and the Bible is growing. When young people are asked to describe Christianity, they use terms such as anti–homosexual, judgmental, hypocritical, old–fashioned, out of touch, insensitive, and confusing.[4] When Americans were asked what they think about the Bible and Christian belief, responses demonstrated their confusion: less than half believe the Bible is fully accurate, 77% believe they must contribute to their salvation, and 74% don't think every sin deserves damnation.[5] Young generations are skeptical about the Bible and confused about Christianity.

Observation 2: Young Americans Are Hyperconnected and Lonely

The internet and digital devices are transforming the culture at a rapid pace. This hyperconnected age is giving rise to a generation of young people that is simultaneously connected and disconnected. Generation Z has abundant access to all kinds of information and people all over the planet. Information, knowledge, and news are widespread and instantly available.

Despite being connected to information and people, this hyperconnected generation is also disconnected from human relationships. With the rise of social media, the nature of human relationships is rapidly changing, as well. As reported by *The Atlantic* magazine, an increasing number of teenagers are reporting severe cases of loneliness, depression, and suicidal thoughts.[6] Another article, published in *Science* magazine, argues that cell phone usage decreases one's ability to read basic social cues.[7] In other words, the more time you spend on your phone, the harder it becomes for you to relate with someone one–on–one in physical, real–life, space. There is a disconnect between their hyperconnected phones and their longing for real human relationships.

Observation 3: Young Americans Have a Growing Interest in the Transcendent

Despite an overall anti–religious sentiment, there remains a deep interest in spiritual things. While fewer adults participate in prayer, Bible study, or religious education, 40% of those who indicate no religious affiliation feel a deep sense of spiritual peace and wellbeing. This number is on the rise and represents a growing hunger for spiritual things.

The popularity of TV shows like *Stranger Things* and *Long Island Medium* demonstrate the fascination with all things mysterious and spiritual, especially the paranormal. In previous generations, there was a closed mind to spiritual things among non–Christians. Today, things are much different. Young non–religious Americans are looking for a spiritual connection with something beyond.

Observation 4: Young Americans Are Embracing a Non–Christian, Desire–Focused Morality

American culture is obsessed with self–fulfillment and self–satisfaction.[8] In this new American spirituality, God is not needed, leaving each person to identify and meet their deepest desires themselves. Personal desire and its fulfillment is the new morality and the new source of confidence. Young people are eager to have any and every desire fulfilled by any means possible. The only moral guardrails are: "as long as it doesn't hurt anyone else." In other words, each person can write their own morality and truth.

This obsession has replaced true Christian spirituality with a therapeutic spirituality that teaches that "the central goal of life is to be happy and to feel good about oneself."[9] A focus on one's happiness and fulfillment is the new gospel of American spirituality.

The Danger of Lukewarm Christian Spiritualism

All Christian believers need to approach American spirituality carefully. When *Star Wars* shows humanity to be spiritual beings, it is correct. We are made to live in communion with some higher power. But we don't get to choose that higher power or shape that higher power to our desires. Following our desires without reference to God's desires for us is idolatry. If we want to seek spiritual things, we must start with the Bible and look to Jesus for clarity and salvation.

How do we respond to people who embrace this spirituality?

Four truths for the spiritual-but-not-religious:

Biblical truth is your best ally.

Christianity offers a relationship with a real savior.

God has revealed himself in creation.

True joy is found in bearing the cross.

08

Four Biblical Truths to Share with the Spiritual–but–Not–Religious

Truth One: Biblical Truth Is Your Best Ally

Young Americans are unfamiliar with the Bible, but the Bible remains your most effective tool for sharing your faith. In fact, the Word of God is the only tool available to us. It is only the word of the gospel that can create and sustain faith: "So faith comes from hearing, and hearing through the word of Christ" (Romans 10:17).

Other verses teach that the Word of God can access, expose, explain, and direct the heart (Hebrews 4:12; cf. 2 Timothy 3:16–17). First Peter 1:2–4 argues that the "knowledge of God" gives us everything we need for life. In other words, God's Word is a sufficient guide in all matters, including helping you grow in and share your faith.

Truth Two: Christianity Offers a Relationship with a Real Savior

The hyperconnected, lonely people you're reaching need to hear this truth. In Matthew 11, Jesus says,

> Come to me, all who labor and are heavy laden, and I will give you rest. Take my yoke upon you, and learn from me, for I am gentle and lowly in heart, and you will find rest for your souls. For my yoke is easy, and my burden is light.

Christianity is about attaching yourself to King Jesus, to his kingdom, to his followers, to his purposes, to his mission, and to his way of life. This is why he says, "Come to me." Christianity is not about keeping a set of rules. Christianity is about worshipping Jesus and obeying him. American Spiritualism offers an empty faith in the individual, the latest fad, or the newest spiritual guru. The spiritual longing that is so strong in younger generations is an opportunity to join them to the creator and Savior of the universe. Point young spiritual people to a Jesus who is known worldwide and expose the emptiness of American spirituality that can only claim some inward feeling that there is something more. God sent Jesus the Son of God to take on human flesh so that humanity will not have to grasp their way along in blind faith.

Truth Three: God Has Revealed Himself in Creation

It's a good thing that people are interested in the transcendent, because evidence for Christianity and God's existence is all around us. Spiritual Americans, especially the younger Generation Z, are interested in and open to spiritual things. God's Word tells us, "The heavens declare the glory of God, and the sky above proclaims his handiwork" (Psalm 19:1). The breadth of the Grand Canyon or the beauty of the Rocky Mountains or the diversity of human culture all point toward the existence of a higher power. Creation elicits an inward longing for the divine.

The very fact that any of us label certain acts as "right" and other acts as "wrong" tells us that there is an objective moral standard (cf. Romans 2:14–15). The point is this: every person knows that God exists and

DEFENDERS OF THE FAITH

CARL HENRY
B.1913 | D.2003

Carl Henry provided intellectual and theological heft to the evangelical movement of the 20th century. He was instrumental in the founding of a number of lasting institutions, organizations, and publications that helped give evangelicals an identity. His massive work, *God, Revelation, and Authority* gave an authoritative articulation of presuppositional apologetics.

IF YOU READ ONE BOOK BY HENRY, MAKE IT: *The Uneasy Conscience of Modern Fundamentalism* (assuming you don't want to dive into all six volumes of *God, Revelation, and Authority*).

knows there are moral standards that they must keep. The problem is that all humans "suppress the truth" (Romans 1:18). Despite this general rejection of the truth, humanity as a whole has a deep longing for God. It is this longing that Paul talked about on Mars Hill in Acts 17 when he proclaimed to the Athenian people the unknown God (Acts 17:23). As we share our faith with others, we need to point to the beauty, mystery, and design of creation. Recent surveys indicate that roughly one in three non–religious Americans agree with general evidences and arguments for God's existence. Because of their spiritual openness and longing, they are open to hearing about "the unknown God," who we know to be the Lord Jesus Christ.

Truth Four: True Joy Is Found in Bearing the Cross

The world tells you that your central purpose in life is to make yourself happy. And to do that, you're encouraged to pursue all your desires with abandon. That is wrong and it will lead you down a path to misery. The central purpose in your life is not to fulfill your desires, but to obey Jesus.

Our goal in life is faithfulness to Christ. We want him to say at the end of our lives, "Well done, good and faithful servant." Yet, the great news is that giving ourselves wholly to Jesus and his kingdom will bring us much more than happiness. It will bring us lasting joy. After he tells his disciples to take up their cross in Matthew 16:24, he goes on to tell them in Matthew 16:25, "For whoever would save his life will lose it, but whoever loses his life for my sake will find it." This is a truth people need to hear.

Don't Let Them Be Content with the Force

We need to take advantage of the deep longing and spirituality that is present in younger generations. They may refuse religion, but they are longing to know and have a relationship with the unknown God we know as Jesus Christ. Don't let them be content with "the force." Jesus Christ, the creator and redeemer of the universe, invites them into a relationship of oneness with him.

ENDNOTES

[1] White, 39.

[2] White, 49.

[3] "Five Trends among the Unchurched," Barna Group, October 9, 2014, https://www.barna.org/barna–update/culture/685–five–trends–among–the–unchurched in White, 49.

[4] David Kinnaman and Gabe Lyons, UnChristian: *What a New Generation Really Thinks about Christianity* (Grand Rapids: Baker, 2007), 28 in White, 83.

[5] "Americans love God and the Bible, are fuzzy on the details" September 27, 2016. Lifeway Research, 2017. http://blog.lifeway.com/newsroom/2016/09/27/americans–love–god–and–the–bible–are–fuzzy–on–the–details/

[6] Jean M. Twenge, "Have Smartphones Destroyed a Generation?," *The Atlantic*, September 2017 Issue.

[7] Y.T. Uhlsa, M. Michikyan, et. al., "Five days at outdoor education camp without screens improves preteen skills with nonverbal emotion cues." *Computers in Human Behavior* 39 (2014): 387–392.

[8] White, 94.

[9] R. Albert Mohler, Jr., "Moralistic Therapeutic Deism––the New American Religion." Christian Post, 18 April 2005.

You don't realize
Jesus is all you
need until Jesus is
all you have.

– Tim Keller

More Than One
Way to God?

BY MARK COPPENGER

09

For a few years in the early 2000s, I lived about a mile from the big Bahá'í Temple in Wilmette, Illinois, north of Chicago. They built it in the afterglow of the 1893–94 World Columbian Exposition – the World's Fair commemorating the 400th anniversary of Christopher Columbus's voyage to the Americas.

The Fair included the first gathering of the Parliament of the World's Religions, whose speakers were Buddhist, Jain, Zen, Bahá'í, Muslim, Christian Science, Swedenborgian, Presbyterian, and Hindu.

Filled with multi–cultural and pluralistic zeal, many were keen to help fund a building for a group saying its devotees "accept, respect, and revere the religion of Abraham, Moses, Krishna, Zoroaster, Buddha, Jesus Christ, Muhammad, and also the sacred traditions of the prophets and teachers of indigenous peoples." The pillars of the temple are decorated with the Christian cross, the Jewish star of David, the Islamic crescent, and the Hindu swastika. And at the top of each is a nine–pointed star, representing the Bahá'í faith and its "many ways to God."

Theological liberals of the universalist camp love this sort of thing, as do secularists and skeptics, who say religion is simply a buffet line of dogmas and ceremonies hatched by people with understandable insecurities and comforting fantasies. But the "more than one way to God" party includes countless amiable laymen of all religious persuasions who are doctrinally and logically challenged.

I've found it everywhere that I've struck up conversations with strangers – in cabs, in coffee shops, or in queues for this or that event. I'll ask them about their faith and then share mine, to which they often respond with something like, "Well, we're all children of the same God." Nice. But nice doesn't cut it here.

The Principle of Non–Contradiction

For one thing, if you don't obey the Law of Non–Contradiction, you talk nonsense. Of course, there's room for paradox, as in the opening of Charles Dickens's *A Tale of Two Cities*: "It was the best of times, it was the worst of times." Literary flair has its place, but that's not what's going on when Christians say that Jesus is the Son of God, and Muslims say he isn't.

I was recently assigned to comment on a paper at our state's philosophical association. In the essay, the author discussed the legal standing of an Indian tribe who believed in the "godhood" of a patch of forest (and so demanded that a logging road not be cut through it). What if a person would say, out of honor and reverence for such indigenous teaching, "Oh, yes, the forest definitely has godhood, and, on the other hand, it doesn't have godhood, since the True God created it"? Where do you go if someone says they're fine with that? The answer is, "Nowhere."

Yahweh says, "Come, let us reason together" (Isaiah 1:18), not "Come, let us talk bizarrely together." And when Paul says, "We seek to persuade men," we don't snap back at him, "No, Paul, we seek to merge conflicting views into a mindless mush so that everybody can be happy."

Blind Men and the Elephant

In this context, some folks like to bring up the story of the blind men and the elephant. In turn, each man touches the elephant's side, tail, tusk, leg, ear, and trunk, and then announces that the beast is like a wall, rope, spear, tree–trunk, leaf, and snake. The point of this story is that each faith makes the best call it can and comes up with part of the truth.

Of course, different religious groups say or do some true or helpful things. Muslims agree with Christians that abortion is wrong. Shinto artists have done aesthetically pleasing work. Native American animists have taught us things about nature care.

But, along with the positives, they also present us with negative declarations and behaviors. Unlike the men with the elephant, they say, in effect, that God is not certain things. And many of those things they deny are a part of Christian orthodoxy.

Ideas Have Consequences

It's often said that ideas have consequences, and it's certainly true of religion. Sad to say, there are those who maintain that the various faiths differ only in incidentals and that, when it comes to the big payoff, they amount to the same thing.

But how could this be when they produce very different things where they predominate in one region or another on earth?

Here's a thought experiment: what if the Pilgrims hadn't landed on (or near) Plymouth Rock, but rather it was a group of Brahmin Hindus? Or Shia Muslims? Or Stonehenge–oriented Druids? Or atheistical Communists? You fill in the blank. Wouldn't our continent have turned out quite differently if it had been developed by people with a caste system? Or by enthusiasts for Sharia Law? Or by sun worshippers?

Would America have produced MIT, founded the Mayo Clinic, and stood forth as the "Arsenal of Democracy" in World War II? Would it have established the New York Philharmonic and fought a bloody Civil War to eradicate slavery? Not likely, for such achievements rely upon a whole range of values that flow from Christian Scripture, such as the rule of law, the dignity of man, esteem for science, a strong work ethic, checks and balances, and compassion.

In contrast, we might look to nations not marked by a strong Judeo–Christian heritage. Think of India, Iran, Soviet Russia, and animist cultures to see what we might well have become. Of course, wherever you look on earth, you find human beings made in God's image, who do some good things.

But, in the aggregate, there are very big differences. Their basic humanity is not in question; rather, their religion, or lack thereof, is the issue. One nation finds a cure for polio while another waits desperately for someone to deliver that serum, and it's no accident that the former has treasured the Bible while the latter has clung to the Koran or the Bhagavad Gita.

"We're All Talking About the Same God"

Yes, I know that some Bible translations render the English "God" as the Arabic "Allah." And yes, American Jehovah's Witnesses say "God," just the same as the Baptists. But what kind of argument is this? If I go to the phone book and see two listings for John Smith, I don't conclude that they're the same guy. Or if two ads proclaim that their product is the "miracle cure" for some malady, do I need to think they're referring to the same thing (especially if one is based on olive oil and the other on mercury)?

I remember the time when an old fellow who attended our Chicago church took me to one of his Alcoholics Anonymous meetings (he was a WWII veteran of Iwo Jima, and he said he thought it was time he "started studying for finals"). These were the folks whose "Twelve Steps" to sobriety included belief in a power greater than themselves. But what does that get you if the "greater power" is an illusion? Is Vishnu really going to help you? What about ISIS? Of course, erroneous beliefs can have a placebo effect, making you feel better or more disciplined. But it's all inside. Not so for Christianity, whose God is real and acts effectually through regeneration, the Holy Spirit, and providence.

No Roads Lead to Bali

Those of the pluralist persuasion like to say that many roads lead to God: "You take yours; I'll take mine; and we'll all end up in the good place." Actually, that's like saying, "All roads lead to Bali." The truth of the matter is that no roads lead to Bali; you have to get there by boat or air. You can't walk there at all.

So it is with salvation; there are no roads, no paths, which humans can walk so that they end up in heaven. It takes a special intervention by God through his Son, Jesus Christ, to bring us to the abundant life and heaven.

More than one way to God?

Christianity teaches that there are no roads,
no paths, which humans can walk so
that they end up in heaven.

Christianity teaches that it takes a special
intervention by God through his Son, Jesus Christ,
to bring us to the abundant life and heaven.

Christianity does not teach that
all religions lead to the same God.

Salvation for the other religions depends
upon the performance of the followers.

A Different Song

This is the key difference between Christianity and the other faiths, and it's reflected in its music. Salvation for the others depends upon the performance of the followers. Eastern religion (Buddhism and Hinduism) focuses on karma and its outworking in one's next reincarnation. India's "untouchables" (Dalits) are justly oppressed because of their missteps in the former life. If they'd only acted better, they might have joined the Braham class, on track to spiral up toward Nirvana and release from the cycle of birth and rebirth.

QUESTION:

If you have a conversation with someone who says that all roads, or all religions, lead to God, how would you respond? Read John 14:6 and Acts 4:12. How would those passages influence your answer?

_____

_____

_____

The Muslim has his "Five Pillars," including a cycle of fasting and feasting during Ramadan, five daily prayers, charitable giving at 2.5%, and a pilgrimage to Mecca. Orthodox Jews are faithful to observe Yom Kippur and Rosh Hashanah, keep kosher, and "sit shiva." For the Reformed Jews, the payoff is good fortune in the upcoming year, and not the hope of eternal rewards. Mormons have their ceremonies and regimens, including Temple sealing, tithing, and missioning.

So, what do these groups have to sing about beyond the possibility of getting through unscathed if your behavior is up to snuff? It's hard to get "Amazing grace, how sweet the sound that saved a wretch like me" out of these systems.

That's why Christianity can be uniquely called a "singing faith," for we have something incredible to sing about. And we do it in so many genres – hymn, cantata, oratorio, gospel, etc. Visit the shops of other religions and you'll find a few sitar–accompanied pieces for Ganesh or Vishnu, some Jewish cantors and klezmer bands at work, and a Muslim boy band from Malaysia. Visit a Christian store, and, as the joke went (before the explosion of online downloads), it's hard to find a book in the midst of so many CDs.

But It's Not Fair!

Wait, billions of people haven't been raised in The Way, so they're goners. How can that be fair? Well, the Bible says that God has revealed himself in a variety of ways, through the handiwork of his created order and through his law written on the heart, not to mention the preached Word.

You might think that people would pick up on the demands of righteousness and realize their own inability to achieve it. If so, they would cry out in repentance for a savior. But they don't. Rather, in the vanity of their souls, they barge ahead with one implausible plan or another.

Let's try one more analogy (albeit a strange one), another island parable, if you will. Imagine that at age 16, everyone on an island is given a 14–foot high truck. Furthermore, there's only one way off the island, a tunnel with a 12–foot clearance. One day, the alarm goes out that a wildfire is sweeping the island and that everyone must leave. Some scoff at the notion that they're in real peril, even though they see smoke in the distance. Others climb into the cabs of their vehicles (i.e., false religions) and make a run for the tunnel. Ignoring the clearance signs, they press on, accelerating all the while, only to crash at the entrance, knocking themselves unconscious.

Both the truck drivers and the stay–behinds behave foolishly, and they perish. They have no good excuse. Only those who follow safety instructions and walk through the tunnel survive.

Similarly, those who humble themselves to walk according to the dictates of sweet gospel reason, whose hearts are tender to divine instruction, and whose eyes are alert to the signs of conscience and manifold evidence, will be saved. There really was just one way.

QUESTION:

List a couple of takeaways from this chapter. What stuck with you or was something you hadn't thought about before? The truth that Jesus is the only way to God should lead us to share the gospel. Who are some people you know who need to hear about Christ?

_____

_____

_____

I am the way, and the truth, and the life. No one comes to the Father except through me.

– Jesus (John 14:6)

PART FOUR

Standing for Christianity

10

Your Mind

BY JEREMY KIMBLE

10

$t$he Christian faith is a delight–filled, comprehensive view on all of life from beginning to end. It provides guidance, structure, truth, morality, and coherence to every part of our existence.

However, there are many who would call Christianity illogical and incoherent. They would put great emphasis on "faith" in the phrase "Christian faith," claiming that everything we believe is mere whimsical wishing, or fantastical delusions meant to help us limp through life.

And yet, when we put the claims of Christianity to the test, we see that it is not a mere leap into nothingness, hoping for the best. Instead, one can look at Christianity and understand it as a "reasoned faith." In other words, the biblical worldview does not call people to check their brains at the door, but invites them to see that, while we live by faith, reason is not opposed to this faith.

In this chapter, my aim is to define both reason and faith and show how they work together within the Christian worldview. What we will eventually see points us back in history to a key phrase: Christianity is "faith seeking understanding." Or to say it another way, the rationality of the biblical worldview is embedded within an informed faith in the biblical God and how he has revealed himself to us.

What Is Reason?

Our reason (or "rationality") can be a complex idea, but it comes down to a basic reality. In a generic sense, reason is the capacity for forming judgments and inferences (i.e., logical interpretations) that align with the way things truly are. Let's break this definition down.

1. Reason is a capacity. It is an ability within human beings, and a skill that can be honed.

2. Reason is for forming judgments and inferences, or deductions. The capacity within us allows us to think logically and to make assessments about the world.

3. Reason forms judgments that align with the way things really are.

In other words, reason allows us to make sense of what we observe in the world.

If that definition wasn't totally clear, maybe some examples will help. If we have six slices of pizza and three people who want to eat some, we can use our reason in the realm of mathematics to figure out how many slices we each get (or it may just come down to who is the fastest!).

Another example might include our powers of observation. We have been told by our parents not to play with fire because it might hurt us. But then we also observe our sibling get burned by touching a hot stovetop. You could use reason to deduce that you should not touch that stovetop right after a dish is cooked, otherwise you would also get burned.

Or one could think of reason in the area of science, in particular the scientific method. As someone studies a certain subject in science, he makes hypotheses, performs tests, makes observations, and then modifies hypotheses based on reasoning through the data.

Examples of reason abound, but the point is that our reasoning capacities are used every day. It is a gift we possess as humans, and it is a gift that should be used for the best possible ends.

QUESTION:

Question: What are some examples of ways you use your ability to reason?

_____

_____

_____

_____

_____

The Role of Reason in Christianity

As Christians, we can and should affirm the good of reason. From a Christian perspective, however, we should take the definition above and nuance it slightly: reason is the God-given capacity for forming *correct, biblical* judgments and inferences that align with the way things truly are.

God is the God who has made all things, including humanity (Genesis 1:1–31). He has specifically made humans in his image with capacities to feel, do, and think in accordance with his ways (Genesis 1:26–28). Reason is a God-given capacity, and one that we as Christians believe should be exercised on a daily basis.

Beyond being made in God's image, God has revealed himself to us in a way that appeals to our reason. We are told that "the heavens declare the glory of God" (Psalm 19:1), and that humanity can see that God exists and that he is powerful through what he has made (Romans 1:18–20). God also gives us consciences, which align with our reasoning capacities to make us aware of what is right and wrong (Romans 2:14–16).

Thus, our reason is valuable as a gift from God since God has revealed himself to us in ways that our reason comprehends. And not only has God shown himself in the natural realm of creation, he has even more specifically shown us who he is in Scripture. This God-breathed Word is profitable for us from beginning to end, as it teaches, reproves, corrects, trains in righteousness, and equips us for every good work (2 Timothy 3:16–17).

However, there is a problem. We were made in God's image in Genesis 1, but almost directly after this the first humans, Adam and Eve, rebelled against God and brought sin and death into the world (Genesis 3:1–19).

As a result, the corruption of the fall has effects even in our reason. In our sinfulness, we take our reasoning capacities and we suppress the truth in creation and in Scripture. Not only that, we exchange the worship of the true God for worshipping idols made in our own image (Romans 1:18–23). As such, in our sinful state, we cannot reason our way to God. Reason only takes us so far. We need something more, and that something more is faith.

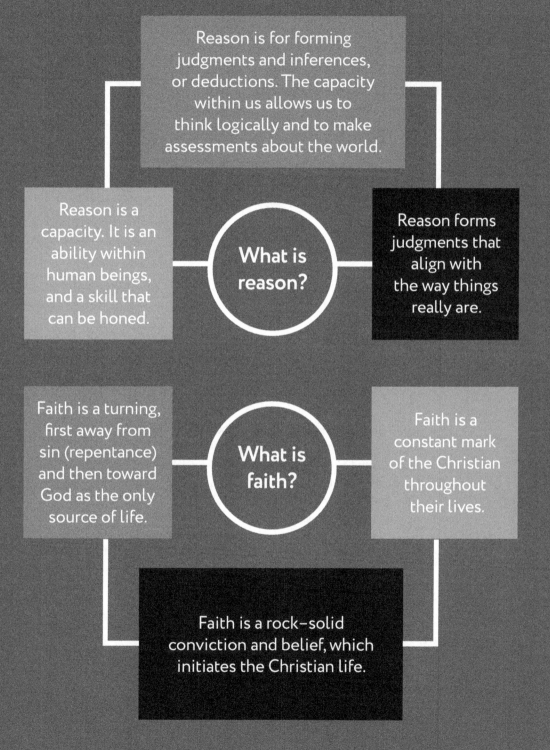

Reason is for forming judgments and inferences, or deductions. The capacity within us allows us to think logically and to make assessments about the world.

Reason is a capacity. It is an ability within human beings, and a skill that can be honed.

What is reason?

Reason forms judgments that align with the way things really are.

Faith is a turning, first away from sin (repentance) and then toward God as the only source of life.

What is faith?

Faith is a constant mark of the Christian throughout their lives.

Faith is a rock–solid conviction and belief, which initiates the Christian life.

What Is Faith?

Faith is another important term that needs to be carefully defined. In a biblical sense, faith is the substance of things hoped for, the conviction of things not seen (Hebrews 11:1). But what are we hoping for, and what unseen things do we have conviction about? This passage requires greater context to make sense of this term. Put more specifically, faith refers to our turning to God, depending on and trusting in the person and work of Jesus Christ to provide forgiveness, righteousness, and eternal life.

Again, a breakdown of this definition would prove helpful.

1. Faith is a turning, first away from sin (also known as "repentance") and then toward God as the only source of life (Acts 17:25).

2. Faith is a rock–solid conviction and belief, which initiates the Christian life (often referred to as "salvation" or "conversion").

3. Faith is a constant mark of the Christian throughout their lives.

We turn to God in dependence and trust because nothing in ourselves could ever get us into right standing with God (Romans 3:10–18). And our dependence and trust is in Jesus, specifically, who he is (fully God and fully man) and what he has done (pay the price for our sins so we can be in right relationship with God the Father). We look to him with active belief and reliance as our Savior (John 3:16), Lord (Romans 10:9–10), and Treasure (John 6:35), satisfied with all that God is for us in Jesus.

True faith in the living God is what allows us to reason correctly, recognizing the greatness of who God is, and how the universe is ordered under him.

Faith Seeking Understanding

Everyone is trying to make sense of the world, attempting to put all the puzzle pieces together. Some people will say there is no God, that all that exists is the universe, what we experience with our senses. Those who adopt this worldview may attack the notion of God because they have never seen or heard him, and so they discount his existence. This is a common view in American culture today as people operate from a culture of skepticism and self–reliance.

Other people may affirm that there is a divine being out there, but they would also say there is no way to know who he really is, so the idea of religion is a pointless pursuit. Some will say that there is a divine power and that he made everything, but he is totally uninvolved in our lives today.

Certain individuals will insist that god is everything and everything is divine in some sense. Still others would affirm that there are many gods and we need to fulfill certain rituals to please each one and live a fulfilling life.

In contrast to all of these views, Christians would affirm and believe in the living God as described in the Bible. And our active love of and faith in God continually seeks a deeper knowledge of God and his world. Some theologians in history have dubbed that last sentence as "faith seeking understanding."

> **True faith in the living God is what allows us to reason correctly, recognizing the greatness of who God is, and how the universe is ordered under him.**

10

The ability to reason is a result of being made in God's image. How does the fall of Genesis 3 affect our ability to reason? (see 2 Corinthians 4:4)

_____

_____

_____

_____

QUESTION:

When people turn to Christ – the true image of God – the Bible says that God's image begins to be restored in us. How does faith in Christ do this? (see 2 Corinthians 3:18 & 2 Corinthians 4:6)

_____

_____

_____

_____

We recognize that God created all things good, including us. We were made in his image, possessing capacities to be in right relationship with God and live in accordance with his ways, and one capacity he gave us is reason. However, when humanity rebels against God, sin and death come to all of humanity. We are conceived in sin (Psalm 51:5), and our capacities to reason, feel, and do are all affected and influenced by this reality. And because of sin, our reason is bent in a self–centered direction, constantly suppressing God–given truth about who he is and what he has made.

Faith in Christ changes us in profound ways, including the way we reason. Through faith we recognize the work of the Spirit through the person and work of Christ, pointing us to the glory of God the Father (Ephesians 1:3–14). In conversion, the spiritual blindness that plagued us is removed and we see clearly the light of the gospel of the glory of God in the face of Christ (2 Corinthians 4:4, 6).

This view of faith allows us to make sense of life as it really is. And as we continue to pursue greater faith in God, this leads to a more insightful knowledge of God and his ways in the world. Specifically, we begin to see that God is before all things, and that in him all things, in every area of life, hold together (Colossians 1:17).

Faith in Christ allows us to be renewed in knowledge after the image of our creator (Colossians 3:10). In other words, the Christian faith best makes sense of life in a logical and empirical sense. We believe and we understand that God is real, active in our world, and that all things come from him, are accomplished through him, and are done for him, so that he would get all the glory (Romans 11:36).

DEFENDERS OF THE FAITH

Os Guinness has unique perspective on the world because of all he's lived through: the Chinese revolution of 1949, an Oxford education, and life in Switzerland and the United States. He continues to travel the world as he lectures in a variety of venues, including speaking engagements with Ravi Zacharias International Ministries. Guinness, who was a student of Francis Schaeffer's, has written more than 30 books.

OS GUINNESS
B.1941

IF YOU READ ONE BOOK BY GUINNESS, MAKE IT:
Fool's Talk: Recovering the Art of Christian Persuasion

10

Conclusion

Questions abound regarding the truthfulness and reliability of the Christian worldview. These questions include whether or not God exists, the trustworthiness of the Scriptures, and inquiries about Jesus' virgin birth, atoning death, and resurrection. The wonderful thing about Christianity — as is shown in the rest of this book — is that we live not by blind faith, but by a reasonable faith.

The evidences and presupposed beliefs stack up in such a way to demonstrate that the Christian faith is true. And this is so not only because we are really wishing that it were true, but because the truth Christianity conveys is the most plausible of all explanations for the realities we see in the universe. Humanity, therefore, is called not to rebel against these truths, but to embrace them by faith, and this provides the pathway for greatest understanding of all of life.

We cannot feel
like Christians or
act like Christians if
we don't think
like Christians.

– Michael Horton

11

Your Witness

BY KEVIN HALL

Oscar Wilde once said, "To live is the rarest thing in the world. Most people exist, that is all." This is a struggle for many who call themselves Christians. We often live in a way that can only be described as survival, leading us to miss the reason we were created.

This should not be the case. For if you know Christ, you have a relationship with the God who created you for himself. We were made for more than mere survival. And this all should result in the Christian's life being an apologetic to the truth of who God is.

Made for More

The first question in the Westminster Confession is, "What is the chief end of man?" The answer is, "To glorify God and enjoy him forever." This is a crucial question, and it is one that people throughout history have asked, wanting to know their purpose in life.

The answer always has to go back to God. God made us so that we would give him glory through a joyful relationship with him. We were made to know God, and we will only be satisfied in a relationship with him.

C. S. Lewis managed to capture this thought that we are made for more by saying, "If I find in myself desires which nothing in this world can satisfy, the only logical explanation is that I was made for another world."

The truth is that we go throughout this world trying to fulfill a desire only God can satisfy. This is true of everyone who was ever created, and it's true of you. Until you come to God through Christ, you will not know the joy for which you were made. This truth is why the psalmist writes, "Taste and see that the Lord is good" (Psalm 34:8a), and why he also testifies, "You made me know the path of life; in your presence there is fullness of joy; at your right hand are pleasures forevermore" (Psalm 16:11).

The truth of why we were made was also uttered by Blaise Pascal, who affirmed, "There is a God-shaped vacuum in the heart of each man which cannot be satisfied by any created thing but only by God the creator, made known through Jesus Christ."

If you know Jesus Christ, you have the truth and answer for which everyone is looking. You have found the treasure of all treasures and the answer to life's most crucial question. The treasure is God himself, a relationship with him through Jesus Christ. This relationship will bring true happiness not only in this life, but for eternity.

How would you answer the question, "What is the purpose of your life?" Do you think this purpose aligns with a verse like 1 Corinthians 10:31? "So, whether you eat or drink, or whatever you do, do all to the glory of God."

_____

_____

_____

_____

A Place to Stand

If you have ever been on a rickety bridge, or tried to stand on something that could not hold your weight, you have understood the importance of a firm foundation. In the Sermon on the Mount, Jesus said this very same thing:

> Everyone who hears these words of mine, and does them, will be like a wise man who built his house on the rock. And the rain fell, and the floods came, and the winds blew and beat on that house, but it did not fall, because it had been founded on the rock. (Matthew 7:24–25)

There are questions that all of humanity faces, and there are many answers, but what you learn very quickly is that many of these answers are not sufficient. They cannot bear the weight of reality. You have to have something – or someone – big enough to give you a foundation, and the world's answers are not big enough.

Christians have answers that the world simply does not. We have a God big enough to carry the weight of the issues we face in this world.

As Francis Schaeffer said concerning the world, there is "no value system strong enough to bear the strains of life." A Christian worldview makes all the difference, and gives you a solid place to stand as you are exposed to the pressures of life.

The Bible says, "His divine power has granted to us all things that pertain to life and godliness, through the knowledge of him who called us to his own glory and excellence" (2 Peter 1:3). All that God has given through his Word and the work of Christ gives you a place to stand, and in having that firm foundation you have what the world does not.

Take a look at the past: civilizations have come and gone, but Christianity remains because its foundation is in the truth. You have been given the truth of God's Word about who you are, who God is, and how you are to respond in all of life's situations. If you know Christ, you have the answers to life that the world does not. This relationship makes you a light to the truth of the gospel where you can shine as lights to the world, and can give hope to those who have none, like a city set on hill (Matthew 5:14).

Drawn to Beauty

Everyone is drawn to beauty. It's part of how we were created, and all true beauty that is found in creation comes from God. So, all beauty reflects God, because God himself is beautiful. This beauty can be seen in God's holiness, love, happiness, and all else that is true of God's character, for it is the sum of all that is true of God.

Being a Christian is not only seeing the beauty of who God is, but also having that beauty reflected in our lives. Dane Ortlund has written, "To become a Christian is to become alive to beauty." To be a Christian is to be in the process of becoming beautified, or becoming more and more like Christ, knowing his goodness and happiness that works its way out in a life of beauty, all for God's glory.

There should be something about our lives that draws people to us, not for who we are by way of personality or achievements, but because we know the one who is truly beautiful. We are called to walk as Christ walked (Ephesians 5:1–2), and in living in relationship with God, we can point the world to the one who is most beautiful as his beauty is reflected in us. This beauty is seen in the way we act, reflecting the character of God in the fruit of the Spirit (Galatians 5:22–23), so that through our conduct those in the world may "see your good deeds and glorify God on the day of visitation" (1 Peter 2:12).

The Apologetic of Our Lives

If someone were to look at your life, would they know you're a Christian? Is there something different about you? Do you stand out from the world around you? Even more specifically, does your life reflect a relationship with God?

One man said, "The unexamined life is not worth living." In this chapter, we want you to examine your life and the reason you are living it. We are created in the image of God, and because of this, we are wired for a relationship with our creator God, and we are made to worship and glorify him who is the definition of truth, beauty, goodness, and happiness. This should make a difference in the way you live, and means that you do not merely exist, but should live life to the full.

One mature Christian's life can say more about God to the world than a library full of theology books. One image the New Testament uses to describe life is that of "walking." What does walking have to do with our lives?

> One mature Christian's life can say more about God to the world than a library full of theology books.

DEFENDERS OF THE FAITH

Ravi Zacharias may be the most well–known Christian apologist today, having defended the faith publicly in more than 70 countries. He founded a ministry, Ravi Zacharias International Ministries, that is active globally as it seeks to challenge false worldviews with the gospel of Christ and to offer eternal life through the gospel message. Zacharias has written dozens of books, including *The End of Reason* and *Jesus Among Secular Gods*.

RAVI ZACHARIAS
B.1946

IF YOU READ ONE BOOK BY ZACHARIAS, MAKE IT: *Jesus Among Other Gods: The Absolute Claims of the Christian Message*

- We are called to be imitators of God, and to walk in love as Christ loved us and gave himself up for us (Ephesians 5:1–2).
- We used to walk as the world does (Ephesians 2:2).
- In being saved by grace there are now good works that God has prepared in advance in which we should walk (Ephesians 2:10).
- We are called to walk in a manner worthy of the calling we have in Christ (Ephesians 4:1; see also Colossians 1:10 and 1 Thessalonians 2:12).
- We are to walk as Christ did (1 John 2:6),
- We should not walk as those who do not know Christ (Ephesians 4:17),
- We are to walk wisely, making the best use of our time (Ephesians 5:17).

If you are a follower of Christ, the way you "walk" should be noticeably different. It is a testimony to the truth as you walk in the light (3 John 4; 1 John 1:7). This kind of walk points to the fact that we were created for something more, that we have a place to stand, and that we have been drawn by beauty and are in turn being made beautiful. This means that we are lights in a dark world pointing to the one for whom we were made, the one who is truth, and the one who is the most beautiful being.

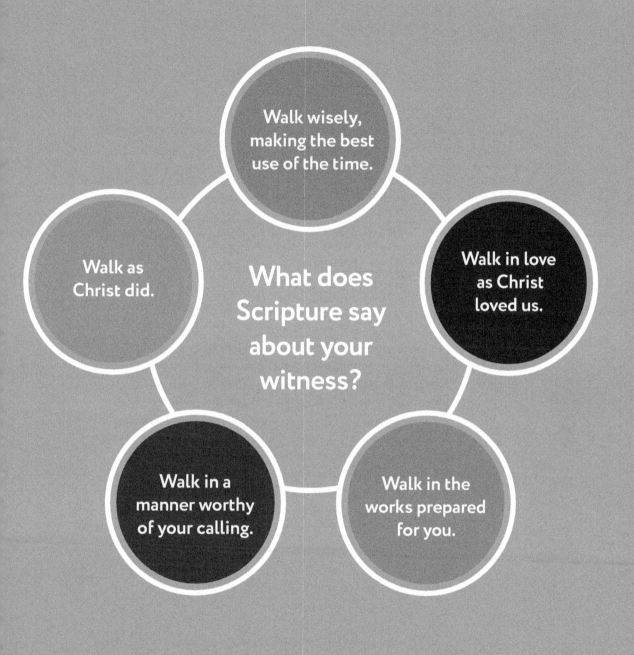

What does Scripture say about your witness?

- Walk wisely, making the best use of the time.
- Walk in love as Christ loved us.
- Walk in the works prepared for you.
- Walk in a manner worthy of your calling.
- Walk as Christ did.

11

Who is an example of someone who lives a compelling Christian life, one that you would want to follow and imitate? What can you do to ensure your "walk" is something others can and should follow?

_____

_____

_____

_____

Talk Your Walk

There is a song I used to sing when I was young: "This little light of mine, I'm gonna let it shine." The gospel should affect the way that you live and should be a testimony to the truth of the gospel. But what we communicate through our lives is not enough to save the lost. People need to hear the truth of who they are before a holy God and what he has done through Jesus Christ to save them.

But those important conversations often begin as you are living out the work of God in your life. It is in living in relationship with the God who created us that we begin to live a life that is an apologetic to the great God we serve. He is the God who saved us and has called us not only to live out that relationship in our walk, but also to proclaim the gospel of salvation in Christ.

Be careful how you live; you will be the only Bible some people ever read.

– William J. Toms

12

Your Worldview

BY DAN DEWITT

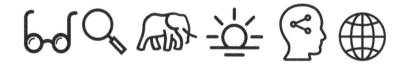

a worldview is simply the way you look at the world. A worldview is like a pair of sunglasses. Once you put them on, they color the way you see everything. But once you have them on you rarely think about them.

Isn't that kind of odd? They make everything look different, but if you're wearing them you don't spend much time thinking about it. Our worldviews are the same way. They are how we look at the world. But most people rarely think about their worldview glasses.

The times we do think about our worldview are a lot like when we might think about our sunglasses. If we get a smudge, or if they are sitting crooked on our nose, or if we walk into a dark room and we have difficulty seeing with them on. In the same way, when our way of looking at the world is challenged, we might step back and begin to consider what we believe about the world.

Finding Your Elephant

If you think about the way you view the world — your worldview — you will discover that you have some foundational things you believe. You base everything else off of these larger things you assume to be true.

One Christian author, James Sire, explains that the foundation of a worldview is like an elephant. He tells the story of a young boy who asks his father what the earth sits on top of. Everything else in the boy's experience has to sit on top of something, so he assumes the same is true for the earth. The father tells his inquisitive son that the earth sits on the back of a turtle.

The boy runs off satisfied to finally know the answer to his burning question. But he quickly returns to ask the obvious follow up question, "What does the turtle sit on top of?" The father tells his that the turtle sits on the back of a camel. Again, the son runs off with a smile on his face.

He then comes back quicker than before to ask the obvious follow up question to the camel answer, "What does the camel sit on top of?" The father immediately responds with the largest animal that comes to mind, an elephant. The son doesn't run off like before, but instead stands there mulling the answer over.

"What's the elephant standing on?" he asks his dad. "Son, it's just elephant all the way down!" his father tells him.

We all have a worldview elephant. We all have a final stopping point for what we believe is the nature of reality, the way the world is. If you were to step back and really look at the way you see the world, you would see that your worldview is built on something big that you assume is true.

The atheist believes the world is all there is. That's his elephant. The Christian believes God exists and that he has revealed himself. These two different ways of seeing the world are attempts at understanding what is ultimate or real. These are ways of getting at a theory that explains everything.

QUESTION:

In addition to the atheist and Christian worldviews, what are some other ways of seeing the world? What are other examples of "elephants" that support the way people view the world?

_____

_____

_____

_____

The Mind of God

When I was in high school, the Walmart in our small town functioned like a shopping mall. It was a place to hang out. But every once in a while, we would go on an adventure. My teenage comrades and I would pile into the most reliable used vehicle owned by one of us at the time and drive 30 miles away to the state capital to visit an authentic, full-orbed, center-of-commercialism-and-materialism, real-deal shopping mall.

These irregular ventures were always a treat. Besides the expected stuff – window shopping at "The Buckle," consuming thousands of calories at Luca's Pizza, and in general trying to project a cool and confident exterior walking through the mall interior – I would usually spend some time sitting cross-legged on the floor in the mall's bookstore, pouring over whatever suited my adolescent pseudo-intellectual mood at the moment. I'll never forget the time that included Stephen Hawking's book, *A Brief History of Time*.

Hawking's discussion of dark matter and dark energy provoked my attention. I acted like I understood what this brilliant scientist was talking about. I didn't. But apparently neither did most people. The book was described as the "least-read-best-seller."

Hawking summarizes the scientist's desire to find a theory of everything in the closing paragraphs of the book:

> "If we do discover a complete theory, it should in time be understandable in broad principle by everyone, not just a few scientists. Then we shall all, philosophers, scientists, and just ordinary people, be able to take part in the discussion of the question of why it is that we and the universe exist. If we find the answer to that, it would be the ultimate triumph of human reason –– for then we would know the mind of God."

This quote has stuck with me since reading it as a teenager. Of course, Hawking wasn't being literal, he doesn't believe in God. He's an atheist. But his quote illustrates something powerful: to get a theory that explains everything, we would pretty much have to know the mind of God.

DEFENDERS OF THE FAITH

LEE STROBEL
B.1952

Lee Strobel was an atheist and a journalist for a number of years before he began investigating the claims of Christianity. He did so because his wife became a Christian and he wanted to dissuade her, but to no avail. His look into the Christian faith not only did nothing to persuade his wife, but he became convinced of the very truth he was trying to disprove. His journalistic approach to apologetic questions led to a series of books, like *The Case for Faith*, *The Case for a Creator*, and many more.

IF YOU READ ONE BOOK BY STROBEL, MAKE IT: *The Case for Christ* (and see the movie that came out in 2017 by the same name)

Everyone	has a worldview.

Knowledge of God	is necessary to understand the world.

The only way to know God	is for God to reveal himself through creation.

We are dependent upon God to explain himself and our world	so we can understand ourselves and our place in his creation.

The Christian Theory of Everything

That is what Christians have the audacity to claim every time they open the Bible. They believe they are learning the mind of God, not by Hawking's "ultimate triumph of human reason," but through God's gracious acts of communicating his love to us.

It is the Christian's conviction that you cannot understand the world unless you understand the creator who made the world, the one who loved the world so much he gave his only Son, so that whoever believes in him might not perish but have everlasting life (John 3:16).

If you miss this, no matter how much you might understand about the physical world, you miss the big picture. You miss what really matters. Jesus said it this way, "What would it profit a man to gain the world and lose his soul?"

Only by knowing God can you understand reality. "The fear of the Lord," King Solomon wrote, "is the beginning of wisdom." Edgar Andrews, emeritus professor of materials at the University of London, seems to echo Solomon's conviction when he explains that the idea of God is necessary for a theory that helps us make sense of the world:

> "A scientist's dream is to develop a 'theory of everything' — a scientific theory that will encompass all the workings of the physical universe in a single self–consistent formulation. Fair enough, but there is more to the universe than matter, energy, space, and time. Most of us believe in the real existence of non–material entities such as friendship, love, beauty, poetry, truth, faith, justice and so on — the things that actually make human life worth living. A true 'theory of everything,' therefore, must embrace both the material and non–material aspects of the universe, and my contention is we already possess such a theory, namely, the hypothesis of God."

The Christian believes, like Professor Andrews, that knowledge of God is absolutely necessary to understand the world. And the only way to know about God, in any meaningful way that might provide insights into reality, is for God to reveal himself to his creation. We are completely dependent upon God to explain himself and our world so that we might understand both ourselves and our place in his creation.

QUESTION:

Why is knowledge of God necessary for understanding the world? How does his role as creator and sustainer of all things influence the way we view the world around us?

_____

_____

_____

_____

_____

_____

_____

_____

> **In addition to offering us a better and more compelling explanation of the world, Christianity has the added benefit of actually being true.**

Our View of the Sun

I began by saying that a worldview is like a pair of sunglasses. It colors everything we see. But there is another way in which the Christian worldview is actually like the sun. It shines light on the world in a way we can understand it.

We can know the sun has risen a couple of different ways. We can wake up to watch the sunrise. Most of us appreciate our sleep too much to do this often. Another way to know the sun has risen is to look across our bedroom and see items like clothes left on the floor or papers or books on the nightstand. In the darkness of the night we couldn't see them, but now, without looking at the sun, we can know the sun has risen, because of the light shining in our rooms.

That's how the gospel works. It shines light on what it means to be human. It explains our world. Like other theories of everything, the Christian worldview is an attempt to explain everything. In addition to offering us a better and more compelling explanation of the world, Christianity has the added benefit of actually being true.

If Christianity should happen to be true – that is to say, if its God is the real God of the universe – then defending it may mean talking about anything and everything.

There are some people — and I am one of them — who think that the most practical and important thing about a man is still his view of the universe.

– G.K. Chesterton

CONTRIBUTORS

Randall Breland serves in the central office as the Director of Communications at Crossings. He is an elder at Kenwood Baptist Church in Louisville, Kentucky and is pursuing a Ph.D. in Old Testament at Southern Seminary. Randall and his wife, Bethany, have two daughters.

Mac Brunson is senior pastor of First Baptist Church, Jacksonville in Florida. He has written and contributed to a number of books, including *Paralyzed by Fear or Empowered by Hope*. He and his wife, Debbie, have three adult children.

Trey Brunson is the director of communication at Southeast Christian Church in Louisville, Kentucky and the executive producer of the film, *Run the Race*. He has served in ministry for nearly 15 years as a pastor and church planter in Texas, Florida, California, and Kentucky. He and his wife, Rachael, have three children.

Mark Coppenger is professor of Christian philosophy and ethics at Southern Seminary and managing editor of the online Kairos Journal. He's written numerous reviews, articles, and books, including Moral Apologetics for Contemporary Christians. He and his wife, Sharon, have three adult children.

Matt Damico is associate pastor of worship at Kenwood Baptist Church in Louisville, Kentucky. He and his wife, Anna, have three children.

Dan Darling is vice president for communications for the Ethics and Religious Liberty Commission of the Southern Baptist Convention and a pastor at Green Hill Church in Mt. Juliet, Tennessee. He's the author of several books, including The Original Jesus, and has written and edited for a number of publications. He and his wife, Angela, have four children.

Dan DeWitt is associate professor of applied theology at Cedarville University and director of the Center for Biblical Apologetics and Public Christianity. He's the author of Christ or Chaos and Jesus or Nothing. He and his wife, April, have four children.

Kevin Hall has been involved in youth and college ministry for more than 25 years and recently completed his Ph.D. in systematic theology at Southern Seminary. Kevin and his wife, Ayemi, have one son.

Timothy Paul Jones is professor of family ministry at Southern Seminary and a pastor at Sojourn Community Church in Louisville, Kentucky. He's written and contributed to many books, including Conspiracies and the Cross and the award–winning Christian History Made Easy. He and his wife, Rayann, have four daughters.

Jeremy Kimble is assistant professor of theological studies at Cedarville University and adult Bible teacher at Grace Baptist Church in Cedarville. He's written and contributed to multiple books, including 40 Questions About Church Membership and Discipline. He and his wife, Rachel, have two children.

R. Albert Mohler Jr. is president of Southern Seminary. He has authored numerous books, including Conviction to Lead, Culture Shift, and most recently The Prayer That Turns the World Upside Down. Mohler hosts two regular podcasts, "The Briefing" and "Thinking in Public." He and his wife, Mary, have two adult children.

Vince Vitale is director of the Zacharias Institute with Ravi Zacharias International Ministries, and was formerly a faculty member at Princeton University and University of Oxford. Vitale has written two books with Zacharias, Why Suffering? and Jesus Among Secular Gods. He's married to his wife, Jo, who also works with RZIM.

Illustrator: Dan DeWitt

Designer: Morgan Carter is a graphic designer located in Louisville, KY. She enjoys working as a freelance designer for organizations across the Southeast.

Editor: Matt Damico

We exist to proclaim the Gospel and to see God transform lives, grow leaders, and partner with the church to the glory of Christ. We are a ministry based in Louisville, Kentucky that offers camps, conference centers, retreats, missions trips, and resources.

Our 600–acre Cedarmore Camp and Conference Center is located in the rolling hills of Bagdad, Kentucky just 45 minutes east of Louisville. Our 100–acre Jonathan Creek Camp and Conference Center is located on Kentucky Lake between Murray and Paducah, Kentucky.

Visit www.gocrossings.org to learn more about our biblically–focused camps, Christ–centered conference centers, and strategic missions trips to Haiti and other international destinations.

As our name suggests, our purpose is centered around youth and family ministry. We exist to equip, edify, and encourage the local church. Our heart is to see the bride of Christ thrive and flourish as they disciple kids, students, and families. We come alongside kids and student pastors, church leaders, parents, and students as they endeavor to grow in Christ and navigate through the many challenges of life and ministry.

How do we accomplish our mission?
- We edify through our ministry–focused blogs, podcasts, and video series.
- We encourage through our array of digital and print resources that we make available to you.
- We equip through our veteran ministry coaches, youth and children's ministry specialists, focused conferences, and training events.

Visit www.youthandfamilyhub.org for more information, to access our resources, to request a speaker, or to contact one of our regional ministry specialist.

Made in United States
Orlando, FL
26 April 2022

17213837R00083